Laurent Godbout

chef at Chez L'Épicier

I hope this book will
help you creating new dishes
Chez l'Épicier style!

Photos: Tango
Prop styling: Luce Meunier

Library and Archives Canada Cataloguing in Publication

Godbout, Laurent

  Laurent Godbout, chef at Chez L'Épicier

  (Tout un chef!)

  Translation of: Laurent Godbout, chef Chez L'Épicier

  1. Cookery. I. Title. II. Series.

TX714.G6213 2004   641.5   C2004-941916-1

For more information about our publications,
please visit our website: **www.edhomme.com**
Other sites of interest: www.edjour.com • www.edtypo.com
www.edvlb.com • www.edhexagone.com • www.edutilis.com

EXCLUSIVE DISTRIBUTORS:

• For Canada
  and the United States:
  MESSAGERIES ADP*
  955 Amherst St.
  Montréal, Québec
  H2L 3K4
  Tél.: (514) 523-1182
  Fax: (514) 939-0406
  * A subsidiary of Sogides ltée

11-2004

© 2004, Les Éditions de l'Homme,
a division of the Sogides Group

© 2003, Tango (photos)

Legal deposit: fourth quarter 2004
Bibliothèque nationale du Québec

ISBN 2-7619-2106-2

Government of Québec – Tax credit for book publishing –
Administered by SODEC – www.sodec.gouv.qc.ca

The publisher gratefully acknowledges the support of the
Société de développement des entreprises culturelles du
Québec for its publishing program.

We acknowledge the financial support of the Government of
Canada through the Book Publishing Industry Development
Program (BPIDP) for our publishing activities.

tout un chef !

Laurent Godbout
chef at *Chez L'Épicier*

Translated from the French by Carl Angers

LES ÉDITIONS DE
L'HOMME

INTRODUCTION

"Live to eat or eat to live?" Many gourmets have a ready answer to this question. For those who really love food and the good life, it can even become a gentle addiction. It's true, I enjoy eating. I especially enjoy tasting. In fact, I particularly appreciate the uniqueness of meals and types of cooking. A bird's eye view of my epicurean life, or that of many others for that matter, might look like a series of meals where no two flavors are alike. During the course of these wine-steeped meals, I had the great pleasure of meeting many chefs. As I am not a cook myself, I simply worship these creative and sensitive spirits that go about turning routine meals into moments of pure pleasure.

Strangely enough, I met Laurent Godbout as is often the case with chefs: briskly, after a meal in a restaurant. Seemingly hidden behind those blond curls, lay talent, personality, and a potful of culinary ideas. At first glance, he seemed like any other chef, both passionate about and preoccupied by his cuisine. After a few words however, it's his distinctive vision of cooking that left an imprint on my mind, like that

RESTAURANT
CHEZ L'ÉPICIER
Nº 311
ST-PAUL EST
MTL
ET BAR À VIN

of a good wine. As chef and restaurant owner, Laurent Godbout defends his culinary creed with fervor: please those who eat at his table in an unorthodox way. Although presentation is important to him, this chef does not try to dazzle us. Nor does he try to capture our attention. Rather, he is a chef with intentions, never an unprincipled food lover.

Laurent Godbout is a young, rising star in the Québécois restaurant business. At 32 years old, he has worked in about 15 prestigious restaurants in Québec, including the Auberge Hatley and the Auberge des Trois Tilleuls, both internationally renown and members of the Relais & Chateaux network. He has also won several prizes at culinary contests. As the happy chef and owner of the Chez L'Épicier Restaurant in Old Montreal, Laurent Godbout constantly reinvents fine cooking with boundless imagination. "In fact, I try to provoke delightful and savory encounters on the plate", as he timidly puts it. His reserved nature, however,

does not conceal a passion for his craft that lights up his face when he talks shop. And when asked to define his style, the answer surges without a doubt: "My cuisine is based on pleasure, a culinary entertainment of sorts".

He leaves more principled discussions to others and favors above all a playful approach, exploring all facets of fine contemporary cuisine. "I think my cooking is rather simple, a flavorful cuisine however. I think my creative side prevails." When you listen to him talk delightfully about guinea fowl supremes stuffed with mangos, salmon stew with violet mustard and fresh mint, Québec lamb tatin with caramelized endives or lychee and strawberry pastry with white chocolate mousse, you understand the passion that drives him. He can communicate that passion, with words as well as on the plate.

That's what you discover when you open the door at Chez L'Épicier: a lived-in place whose apparent simplicity is natural and self-evident. "We wanted to create a friendly atmosphere, where you can feel at home", explains the Chef. "We don't want to be old-fashioned at all costs, nor do we feel we have to be modern. Past and future come together to better serve the present." On each table, an ornamental lemon suggests a Japanese outline. The water bottles are old-fashioned glass milk bottles, evoking rural Québécois origins.

Nevertheless, he himself could not have foreseen such a success when he made his career choice. As a 16-year-old teenager from the Mégantic Lake region, he played his future by tossing heads or tails between woodworking and cooking. As is the case with many chefs around the world, nothing seemed to predispose the young man to make dining pleasures the mission of an entire life. "My mother cooked like any other mother, he remembers, but

no one in my family was in the restaurant business. I only had a vague idea of what it was. Most of all, I didn't realize just how many hours of work this job requires!" No regrets, however, in his voice. On the contrary, his love of his work transpires at every word. He is proud of his success and the team that assists him in the pursuit and realization of a dream.

Stopping at nothing, he has recently marketed a range of homemade products bearing the L'Épicier label. He features maple syrup flavored with various essences, and maple- or ginger-flavored vinegar. In addition, he sells oils and salad dressings that are well-kept secrets. Next thing you know, he'll be selling homemade marshmallows…

Who knows what this man has in store for us in the future. Whatever it is, you can bet he's already working on it. At this very moment, in fact, he's probably creating something unexpected. That is the real Laurent Godbout, as his close friends have come

to know him: a man driven by chance encounters, love of food, curiosity, principles and... the unexpected. All this combined with a generous desire to share.

Laurent Godbout, the chef, the businessman, the family man and the gourmet, is pleased to offer you his first book of recipes. He gives you access to fifteen years of research and gastronomic experience and shares a passion that calls on just about all five senses: once you have touched, seen, smelled and tasted one of these 65 delights, you may even be able to hear a divine melody in your ear...

With all his best regards, here he is, the Laurent Godbout that I know. And this book, as tasteful as it is, is a real gift for me, a smorgasbord of wild delights that make for wonderful chance encounters. As Laurent Godbout would put it, it's the moment that counts.

FRÉDÉRIC BLAISE

RESTAURANT

CHEZ L'ÉPICIER
Nº311
ST-PAUL EST
MTL
ET BAR À VIN

Spicy Vegetable Broth
With Pickled Cucumbers

Serves 4

You can buy citronella, lime leaves, shrimp paste and fish sauce in Asian grocery stores. Galanga is a big, knotty rhizome used in Thai and Indonesian cuisine. Its spicy flavor can replace ginger in many recipes.

Broth: Shell the shrimp and put them in the refrigerator. Make sure you keep the shells. Heat the oil in a saucepan. Add the shells, the vegetables and the citronella. Sweat the ingredients over high heat while stirring constantly. Add the shrimp paste, lime leaves, coriander and ginger. Pour in the wine, fish sauce and broth. Simmer for 30 min. Filter the mixture. Season to taste by adding chili if the broth is not spicy enough or chicken stock if it's too spicy. Put aside.

Pickles: Cut the cucumber in two lengthwise and remove the seeds with a spoon before cutting it into sticks. Bring the vinegar, sugar and chili to a boil. When the liquid has cooled, add the cucumbers and let them marinate in the refrigerator.

Patties: Place the vegetables in a bowl. Mix the shrimp, egg, flour and cream in the blender for 40 seconds until minced. Pour over the vegetables. Add cayenne pepper, coriander, salt and pepper and stir well. Shape into patties and keep them in the freezer for 30 min.

INGREDIENTS

BROTH
- Shells of shrimp used to make the patties
- 1 tablespoon of oil
- 70 g ($^1/_3$ cup) carrots, sliced
- 1/2 teaspoon chili peppers, thinly sliced
- 50 g ($^1/_4$ cup) onions, thinly sliced
- 1 stalk of celery, thinly sliced
- 50 g ($^1/_4$ cup) leeks, thinly sliced
- 1 citronella stick, thinly sliced
- 80 g ($^1/_3$ cup) shrimp paste
- 5 lime leaves
- 1/2 sprig of coriander
- 1 teaspoon fresh ginger, chopped
- 75 ml ($^1/_3$ cup) white wine
- 1 teaspoon fish sauce
- 1 liter (4 cups) chicken stock

PICKLES
- 1 English cucumber, peeled
- 60 ml ($^1/_4$ cup) white vinegar
- 60 g ($^1/_4$ cup) sugar
- Pinch of fresh chili

PATTIES

- 1 tablespoon green onions, finely chopped
- 1 tablespoon red onions, finely chopped
- 1 tablespoon green peppers, finely chopped
- 1 tablespoon red peppers, finely chopped
- 16 shrimp (26 to 30 per kg)
- 1 egg yolk
- 1 teaspoon flour
- 1 tablespoon heavy cream (35 %)
- 1 teaspoon cayenne pepper
- 1 tablespoon fresh coriander, chopped
- Freshly ground salt and pepper

BATTER

- 60 g (⅓ cup) flour
- 1 egg
- 75 ml (⅓ cup) milk
- 80 g (⅔ cup) white sesame seeds
- Frying oil

Batter: Put the flour in a medium bowl, the egg and the milk in a second bowl and the sesame seeds in a third bowl. Flour the patties, dip them in the egg preparation and finally roll them in the sesame seeds. Put aside in the refrigerator. Heat a deep fryer to 180°C (350°F) and cook the patties 8 to 10 min. (If you don't have a deep fryer, you can fry them in a pan and finish them in the oven at 180°C (350°F) for 8 min.)

To Serve: Heat the broth until very hot. Serve with a shrimp patty and pickles.

Cream of Corn With Lobster Oil

Serves 4

You can replace the corn with sweet potatoes to create another original recipe.

Cream of Corn: In a medium saucepan, melt the butter over high heat until lightly colored. Add the onions, lower the heat to medium and fry until they begin to brown. Add the corn and sweat for 2 min. Add the chicken stock and simmer for 10 min. Mix in the blender at high speed. Filter the mixture using a China cap strainer to remove the corn peels. Put the soup back into the saucepan. Add the cream, turmeric, salt and pepper.

Lobster Oil: Separate the flesh from the shells of the lobsters. Let the shells dry in the oven at 120°C (250°F). Place the dried shells in a saucepan, heat and add the oil. Using a thermometer, keep the oil temperature at 27°C (80°F) for 1 hour. Filter the oil through an oil or coffee filter.

Topping: In a frying pan, melt the butter over high heat until lightly colored. Add the green onions and stir for 2 min. Add the tomatoes and stir for 1 min. Add the lobster oil and remove from heat.

To Serve: Serve the cream of corn in heated bowls. Put 1 tablespoon of topping in the middle and a drizzle of lobster oil all around.

INGREDIENTS

CREAM OF CORN
- 1 teaspoon butter
- 1 onion, finely chopped
- 380 g (2 cups) corn
- 250 ml (1 cup) chicken stock
- 60 ml (¼ cup) cream
- 1 teaspoon turmeric
- Salt and pepper

LOBSTER OIL
- 2 cooked lobster shells
- 200 ml (¾ cup + 1 tablespoon) canola oil

TOPPING
- 1 teaspoon butter
- 2 tablespoons green onions, chopped
- 45 g (¼ cup) tomatoes, diced
- 60 ml (¼ cup) lobster oil

Cauliflower Purée, Beurre Noisette, Orange and Baby String Bean Salad

Serves 4

INGREDIENTS

CAULIFLOWER PURÉE

- 60 g (¼ cup) unsalted butter
- 1 medium onion, diced
- 1 small cauliflower, diced
- 500 ml (2 cups) chicken stock
- 75 ml (⅓ cup) heavy cream (35 %)
- Salt and pepper

ORANGE AND BABY STRING BEAN SALAD

- 1 orange
- 80 g (⅓ cup) sugar
- 1 teaspoon water
- ½ teaspoon fresh ginger, chopped
- 16 baby string beans, cut in two along the length and the width

PREPARATION

If you want to reduce your cholesterol intake, you can omit the beurre noisette.

Cauliflower Purée: In a medium saucepan, melt 1 tablespoon of butter over high heat until lightly colored. Add the onions and lower the heat to medium. Fry the onions until they begin to brown. Add the cauliflower and sweat for 2 min. Add the stock and simmer for 20 min. Mix in the blender at high speed and return it to the saucepan. Add the cream. In another pan, heat the rest of the butter until hazel colored and add to the purée. Stir, taste and add salt and pepper to taste.

Orange and Baby String Bean Salad: Peel the orange including the skin and fashion the slices into supremes by cutting between each membrane with a knife. Set aside in a bowl and press the remaining parts to extract a maximum amount of juice. Put the sugar and water in a saucepan and heat over high heat to obtain a caramel texture. When it starts to color, add the orange supremes and juice. Simmer 2 min. Add the ginger and string beans and stir well.

To Serve: Pour the purée into heated bowls and garnish with a few spoonfuls of salad and caramel.

Creamy Eggplant Pulp, Smoked Salmon Roll and Curried Cottage Cheese

Serves 4

You can serve this soup cold during the summer.

Pulp: Wrap the eggplant in aluminum foil and place in oven at 200°C (400°F). Meanwhile, melt the butter in a saucepan. Add the onions and fry lightly for 2 min. Add the flour and stir well. Add the stock and the cream. Bring to a boil and cook for 20 min. Mix in the blender and return it to the saucepan. Using a spoon, peel the skin off the eggplant and place it in the soup. Break up the eggplant by whisking vigorously until lumps of only 1 to 2 cm (½ to ¾ in.) remain. Keep warm.

Smoked Salmon Roll: Fry the onions in butter for 3 min. over medium heat. Place in a bowl. Add the cheese, dill, salt and pepper and stir. Spread this preparation on slices of salmon and roll to make a sausage. Slice into 4 slices.

To Serve: Combine the olive oil and the curry. Pour the soup into bowls and drop a slice of roll in each. Flavor with curry oil and serve.

INGREDIENTS

PULP
- 1 medium eggplant
- 2 tablespoons butter
- 50 g (¼ cup) medium onions, diced
- 2 tablespoons flour
- 1 liter (4 cups) chicken stock
- 75 ml (⅓ cup) heavy cream (35 %)

SMOKED SALMON ROLL
- 1 tablespoon red onions, finely diced
- 1 knob of butter
- 75 ml (⅓ cup) cottage cheese
- 1 teaspoon fresh dill, chopped
- Freshly ground salt and pepper
- 4 large slices of smoked salmon

TO SERVE
- 2 tablespoons olive oil
- ¼ teaspoon Madras curry

Cream of Caramelized Onion
With Old Cheddar,
Anchovy Butter Croutons

INGREDIENTS PREPARATION

SOUP
- 6 onions, peeled and thinly sliced
- 2 tablespoons butter
- 75 ml (⅓ cup) port
- 500 ml (2 cups) veal stock
- 75 ml (⅓ cup) heavy cream (35 %)
- Freshly ground salt and pepper

CROUTONS
- 1 whole wheat baguette
- 60 g (¼ cup) unsalted butter
- 6 anchovy fillets
- 2 teaspoons fresh parsley

TO SERVE
- Old cheddar, grated

You can prepare extra portions of soup and keep them in the freezer for five months. Plan to make extra croutons. People will ask for more. If you have leftover anchovy and parsley butter, it will keep in the refrigerator up to two months in a sealed container. Tell your guests to stir the cheese in with a spoon, then sip the cream of onion while nibbling on a crouton.

Soup: In a saucepan, fry the onions in butter until they color without browning. Add the port and simmer 1 min. Add the veal stock and cream. Cook for 20 min. over medium heat. Stir often to avoid burning. Mix the soup in the blender to obtain a smooth, creamy texture. Pass the preparation through a sieve. Season to taste and put aside.

Croutons: Using a serrated knife, cut four 1 cm (½ in.) slices of baguette on a slant. Heat the oven to 200°C (400°F). Soften the butter in the food processor 1 min. Add the anchovies and parsley and mix another minute. Butter the slices of bread with this butter. Place the croutons on a baking sheet. Bake in the oven on the middle rack about 7 min. until lightly colored.

To Serve: Pour the hot soup into bowls. Add the grated cheese in the middle. Place the crouton on top and serve.

Cream of Turban Squash, Chestnut Purée With Cinnamon and Liquid Mascarpone

Serves 4

You can purchase canned sugar-free chestnut purée that is
ready to use.

Soup: Fry the butter in a saucepan. Add the onions and sweat for 2 min.
Add the squash. Add the stock and cream. Cook for about 30 min. Mix in
the blender and put aside.

Chestnut Purée: Preheat oven to 230°C (450°F). Using a knife, make a
lengthwise incision in the chestnuts. Place in the oven for about 15 min.
until they are all open, checking from time to time if they are done. Let
cool at room temperature before peeling them. Mix in the food processor
with the butter, salt, pepper and cinnamon to obtain a smooth creamy
texture. Put aside.

Ravioli: Bring the cream to a boil. Add the mascarpone and stir. Refrigerate
15 min. Lay 4 leaves of dumpling on the table. Put ½ tablespoon of
mascarpone in each center. Brush the edges with egg yolk. Place
another leaf of dumpling on top. Carefully seal the edges and put aside.

Before Serving: Boil some water and poach the mascarpone raviolis 3 min.
Heat the soup and pour into bowls. Heat the purée 1 min. in the
microwave oven and put 1 tablespoon in each bowl. Add the ravioli and
serve.

INGREDIENTS

SOUP
- 1 tablespoon butter
- 1 onion, thinly sliced
- 400 g (2 cups) turban squash flesh, peeled and diced
- 750 ml (3 cups) chicken stock
- 125 ml (½ cup) heavy cream (35 %)

CHESTNUT PUREE
- 12 chestnuts
- 1 tablespoon butter
- Freshly ground salt and pepper
- Pinch of fresh cinnamon

RAVIOLI
- 1 tablespoon heavy cream (35 %)
- 2 tablespoons mascarpone
- 8 pasta dumplings
- 1 egg yolk

RESTAURANT
CHEZ L'ÉPICIER
N°311
ST-PAUL EST
MTL
ET BAR À VIN

Cucumber Caesar's Salad With
Feta Croutons and Black Beans

Serves 4

You can replace the feta croutons with
miniature Parmesan fondues.

Feta Croutons: Bread the feta cubes with corn flour and put aside.

Dressing: Mix all the ingredients (except the canola oil) in the blender
1 min. Gently add the canola oil to obtain a creamy mayo-type sauce.

To Serve: Cut the lettuce into pieces. Cook the black beans 20 min. in salted
boiling water. Drain and cool. Fry the feta croutons in oil for about 1 min.
Combine the lettuce and cucumbers with a little dressing. Place in the
middle of the plate and garnish with warm croutons and black beans.

PREPARATION

INGREDIENTS

FETA CROUTONS
- 75 g ('/₄ cup) feta cheese, cut into
  1 cm ('/₂ in.) cubes
- 60 g ('/₃ cup) corn flour

DRESSING
- 1 egg yolk
- 1 teaspoon capers
- 1 teaspoon parsley
- 2 teaspoons lemon juice
- 3 anchovies
- 1 tablespoon Parmesan cheese
- '/₂ teaspoon garlic, chopped
- 3 drops Worcestershire sauce
- 1 drop Tabasco sauce
- Pepper
- 1 tablespoon Dijon mustard
- 300 ml (1'/₄ cup) canola oil

TO SERVE
- 4 leaves of Romaine lettuce, well washed
- 50 g ('/₄ cup) black-eyed peas
- 1 liter (4 cups) water
- 1 teaspoon salt
- Frying oil
- 1 cucumber, cut into thin slices lengthwise

Warm Vegetable and Pancetta Salad With Pine Nuts and Goat Cheese Pesto

Serves 4

Use bigger servings to turn this recipe into a main dish rather than a side dish.

Pesto: Mix all the ingredients in the food processor to obtain a smooth pesto. Put aside in the refrigerator.

Salad: Blanch the onions, carrots, broccoli, peppers and potatoes in salted boiling water from 7 to 8 min. Bake the pancetta in the oven at 190°C (375°F) on parchment paper until it is quite crispy. Place on a paper towel to remove excess fat.

Dressing: Blend all the ingredients 1 min. in the blender and put aside.

To Serve: Heat a pan over high heat with a little extra virgin olive oil. Cook the vegetables for 6 min. over medium heat. Add the pancetta and cook 2 more min. Meanwhile, season the mixed salad with a little dressing and serve in individual bowls. Stir the vegetables often to avoid burning them. Add the pine nuts. Deglaze with a heaping spoonful of pesto and 2 tablespoons of dressing. Stir well. Spread the goat cheese over the green salad and cover with the heated vegetables.

INGREDIENTS

PESTO
- 1 sprig of basil
- 1 clove of garlic
- 125 ml (½ cup) olive oil
- 2 tablespoons Parmesan cheese
- 2 tablespoons of lime juice
- 2 tablespoons pine nuts, roasted

SALAD
- 12 cippolini onions, peeled
- 12 pearl onions, peeled
- 12 carrots with leaves, peeled
- 1 head broccoli, cut into small flowerets
- 12 miniature peppers, halved
- 8 small round potatoes, quartered
- 12 slices of pancetta

DRESSING
- 125 ml (½ cup) olive oil
- 1 clove of garlic
- 1 gray shallot
- Juice of one lemon
- 2 tablespoons balsamic vinegar
- 1 twig of rosemary
- 1 teaspoon tamari
- 1 tablespoon pesto

TO SERVE
- 60 ml (¼ cup) extra virgin olive oil
- 1 package of mesclun (mixed green salad)
- 4 tablespoons pine nuts
- 4 slices of goat tomme, 1 cm (½ in.) thick

Goat Cheese Mousse, Aragula and Cherry Tomato Salad, Balsamic Caramel and Corn Bread French Toast With Olive Oil

GOAT CHEESE MOUSSE
- 115 g (¾ cup) goat cheese
- 175 ml (¾ cup) semi-whipped cream
- 2 gelatine leaves
- 1 tablespoon cream
- 8 basil leaves

ARAGULA AND CHERRY TOMATO SALAD
- 80 g (1½ cup) aragula leaves, washed
- 12 cherry tomatoes, halved
- 60 ml (¼ cup) olive oil
- Juice of one lemon
- Fleur de sel
- Freshly ground pepper

BALSAMIC CARAMEL
- 75 ml (⅓ cup) balsamic vinegar, at least 8 years old

CORN BREAD FRENCH TOAST
- 1 corn cake recipe (p. 57)
- 1 egg
- 60 ml (¼ cup) milk
- 2 tablespoons olive oil

PREPARATION

If you find the taste of goat cheese too strong, try mountain goat cheese or Quark.

Goat Cheese Mousse: Leave the goat cheese at room temperature for 20 min. Blend in food processor to obtain a creamy cheese. Place in a bowl and add the semi-whipped cream.

• Let the gelatine leaves soften in a little water. Meanwhile, heat the cream in the microwave oven, then add the well wrung gelatine leaves. Stir to obtain a watery consistency. Stir the goat cheese briskly, add to the gelatine and place in a pastry bag.

• Line small ramequins or molds with cellophane wrap. Drop a little cheese on the bottom of each. Garnish with a basil leaf. Drop a little more cheese and alternate until full. Keep in the refrigerator 2 hours.

Aragula and Cherry Tomato Salad: When you are ready to serve, combine all the salad ingredients in a bowl.

Balsamic Caramel: In a saucepan, bring the balsamic vinegar to a boil over high heat until it reduces by half. Keep in a small pot.

Corn Bread French Toast: Cut the corn cake into 1 cm (½ in.) thick slices. Beat the egg and milk using a whisk. Soak the cake slices in this mixture. Put the olive oil in a frying pan over medium-high heat. When it starts to smoke, remove the cakes from the mixture and brown as you would for French toast.

To Serve: Take the goat cheese mousse out of the refrigerator 20 min. before serving. Immediately remove from the mold and remove the cellophane wrap. Place on individual plates and garnish with salad. Pour the balsamic caramel in a circle around the mousse and serve with a slice of French toast.

Tomato and Artichoke Mousseline Layers With Sour Cream Ravigote

Serves 4

SOUR CREAM RAVIGOTE
- ½ teaspoon capers, very finely chopped
- ½ teaspoon green onions, very finely chopped
- ½ teaspoon parsley, very finely chopped
- 1 teaspoon lemon juice
- 75 ml (⅓ cup) sour cream
- Freshly ground salt and pepper

MOUSSELINE
- 4 big, very fresh artichokes
- 1 liter (4 cups) water
- 1 teaspoon salt
- 60 ml (¼ cup) olive oil
- 1 lemon, quartered
- 2 gelatine leaves
- 125 ml (½ cup) semi-whipped cream
- Freshly ground salt and pepper

TOMATOES
- 4 yellow tomatoes
- 4 red tomatoes
- 4 orange tomatoes
- Freshly ground fleur de sel and pepper
- 12 herb shoots
- 12 artichoke chips (optional)

Spread the tomatoes on slices of warm garlic bread, then spread the mousseline on top for a new wave bruschetta effect. You can make artichoke chips by peeling an artichoke as you would for the mousseline. Cut it into thin slices and fry them. Add salt and serve.

Sour Cream Ravigote: Combine capers, green onions, parsley, lemon juice and sour cream. Add salt and pepper and keep in the refrigerator.

Mousseline: Using a serrated knife, cut off the outer rim and leaf tops on the artichokes to remove as many fibers and leaves as you can. When you reach the base, cut the top part and remove the hairy choke using a spoon. Add salt, olive oil and lemon juice to the water and bring to a boil. Cook the artichokes about 20 min. When you poke the tip of a knife into the base, it should come easily. Drain and mix in the food processor to obtain a very smooth purée. Pass the purée through a sieve. Heat one quarter of the purée in the microwave oven. Soften the gelatine in cold water. Drain well and combine with the purée straight from the microwave oven. Add to the remaining artichoke purée and set aside at room temperature for a few minutes before adding the semi-whipped cream. Stir no more than a few seconds to obtain a uniform mousseline. Add salt and pepper and pour into a container. Keep at least 4 hours in the refrigerator.

Tomatoes: Cut the tomatoes into slices of about 0.5 cm (¼ in.). Add salt and pepper. Place the yellow tomatoes in individual plates. Using a spoon, spread a thin layer of mousseline on top. Keep adding levels by using red and then orange tomatoes. Serve the ravigote in a circle around the tomatoes and decorate the top with a few herb shoots and artichoke chips.

Red Onion Salad With Coriander, Prosciutto Candies, Corn Panacotta and Curried Caramel

4 portions

For better results, use gelatine leaves if possible.

Panacotta: Heat the corn and milk about 20 min. over medium heat. Mix in the food processor to obtain a smooth purée. Pass the mixture through a sieve. Soak the gelatine 2 min. in cold water and use your hands to carefully wring out all the water. Place the gelatine in the warm cream of corn and stir well. Let stand about 20 min. at room temperature. Meanwhile, whip the cream until about three quarters stiff. Add salt, pepper and the cream of corn. Pour into a mold and keep in the refrigerator 4 hours.

Red Onion Salad: Soak the vermicelli in water. Cut the aragula and coriander leaves, wash thoroughly and keep them in the refrigerator to maintain crispness. Combine the onions, olive oil, lemon juice, wine and honey. Add salt and pepper and let marinate 1 hour.

Prosciutto Candies: Cut the slices of prosciutto in two, then cut them lengthwise into 3 little strips. Put aside. Cook the garlic cloves about 10 min. in salted water. Repeat this procedure twice, changing the water each time. Drain the cloves. Heat the milk, drop in the garlic cloves and cook about 10 min. Drain. Place in the food processor along with the butter, salt and pepper and reduce to a purée. Place a drop of garlic purée on the bottom of a prosciutto strip. Fashion into a triangle and seal. Make sure the purée stays inside. Heat the frying oil and fry the candies 2 min. Drain on a paper towel and put aside.

Curried Caramel: Bring the sugar and wine to a boil to obtain a light caramel. When it is lightly colored, add the curry and lemon juice. Cook 2 min. Add the butter, turn off the heat and let cool.

To Serve: Take the panacotta out of the refrigerator. Stir the onions, aragula and coriander thoroughly. Assemble the red onion salad on the plate with the panacotta. Garnish with curried caramel and finish with the prosciutto candies.

INGREDIENTS

PANACOTTA
- 50 g (¼ cup) corn
- 75 ml (⅓ cup) milk
- 1 1/2 gelatine leaves
- 60 ml (¼ cup) whipping cream
- Salt and pepper

RED ONION SALAD
- ¼ package of rice vermicelli
- 1 liter (4 cups) water
- Aragula
- Fresh coriander leaves
- 2 red onions, sliced into thin rings
- 75 ml (⅓ cup) olive oil
- 2 tablespoons lemon juice
- 2 tablespoons white wine
- 1 teaspoon honey
- Freshly ground salt and pepper

PROSCIUTTO CANDIES
- 6 prosciutto slices
- 12 garlic cloves
- 1 liter (4 cups) salted water
- 125 ml (½ cup) milk
- 1 tablespoon butter
- Salt and pepper
- Frying oil

CURRIED CARAMEL
- 60 g (¼ cup) sugar
- 1 tablespoon white wine
- 1 teaspoon curry
- Juice of one lemon
- 1 knob of salted butter

Asparagus, asparagus...

Serves 4

Try your hand preparing this recipe with other fresh
garden vegetables. Make a bigger batch of olive powder
that you can use in other recipes according to your tastes.
This powder will keep three months in a sealed container
at room temperature.

Cream of Asparagus: In a medium-sized saucepan, melt the butter until
hazelnut colored. Add the onions and asparagus tips. Fry 2 min. over
medium heat. Add the stock and cook 20 min. Add the cream and mix
in the blender to obtain a very smooth cream.

Smoked Salmon Butter: Mix the smoked salmon, butter and pepper in a food
processor until the consistency is smooth and creamy. Place a sheet of
cellophane wrap on the table and spread the smoked salmon butter on top
using a spatula. Roll into a sausage and place in the refrigerator about
20 min.

Salad: Bring the water and salt to a boil and cook the asparagus al dente
4 to 5 min. Immediately plunge them in cold water to preserve their color.
Peel the oranges including the skin and use a knife to remove the slices.
Combine the oranges, asparagus, olive oil and pepper. Add the fleur de sel
at the very end.

Olive Powder: Dry the olives 4 hours in the oven at 80°C (175°F), until they
are quite dry. Use the food processor to reduce to a very fine powder.

Sautéed Asparagus: Cook the asparagus al dente in salted boiling water.
Season the foie gras well. Whip the cream with the mustard to obtain a
heavy whipped cream. Put aside. Slowly heat the cream of asparagus.
Heat a frying pan and fry the foie gras 30 seconds on each side. Remove
the foie gras from the pan and put aside on a plate. Place the asparagus in
the same pan, add salt and pepper. Coat the asparagus well with the foie
gras butter. Place on the plate with the foie gras.

To Serve: Pour the cream of asparagus into espresso cups. Cut the smoked
salmon butter into thin slices and place a slice in each cup. Serve the salad
on plates. Pour a little olive oil and lemon juice on top and finish with a
little olive powder. Add the asparagus and foie gras. Add the whipped
cream and serve.

INGREDIENTS

CREAM OF ASPARAGUS
- 1 tablespoon butter
- 25 g (⅛ cup) onions, thinly sliced
- 80 g (⅓ cup) asparagus tips, chopped
- 175 ml (¾ cup) chicken stock
- 2 tablespoons heavy cream (35 %)

SMOKED SALMON BUTTER
- 2 tablespoons smoked salmon
- 2 tablespoons softened butter
- Freshly ground pepper

SALAD
- 1 liter (4 cups) water
- ½ teaspoon salt
- 12 wild or young asparagus, peeled
- 2 oranges
- 2 tablespoons extra virgin olive oil
- Freshly ground pepper
- Fleur de sel
- Lemon juice

OLIVE POWDER
- 10 Kalamata olives, pitted

SAUTÉED ASPARAGUS
- 8 asparagus spears, peeled
- 1 liter (4 cups) water
- ½ teaspoon salt
- 4 2.5 cm (1 in.) cubes of foie gras
- Salt and pepper
- 60 ml (¼ cup) heavy cream (35 %)
- 1 tablespoon hot Dijon mustard

Portobello Spring Rolls With
Sun-dried Tomatoes and Spicy Peanut Sauce
Serves 4

INGREDIENTS

SPRING ROLLS

- 1 package of rice vermicelli
- 1.5 liters (6 cups) water
- 2 tablespoons butter
- 1 onion, thinly sliced
- 3 portobello mushrooms, thinly sliced
- 1 garlic clove
- 50 g (¼ cup) sun-dried tomatoes
- 16 Kalamata olives, pitted
- 6 g (¼ cup) basil
- 8 layers of spring roll dough
- 2 tablespoons water
- 2 tablespoons flour
- Frying oil

SPICY PEANUT SAUCE

- 120 g (½ cup) creamy peanut butter
- 75 ml (⅓ cup) water
- 1 tablespoon oyster sauce
- 5 drops Tabasco sauce
- 1 teaspoon sugar
- 1 small garlic clove, chopped

PREPARATION

Make several small rolls and keep them in the freezer for emergencies.

Spring Rolls: Soak the vermicelli in water for about 30 min. Meanwhile, in a frying pan, melt the butter over medium-high heat. Add the onions and cook until lightly caramelized. Add the Portobello mushrooms and sauté. Add the garlic, sun-dried tomatoes and olives and cook for 1 min. Add the basil, transfer into a bowl and put aside.

• Separate the layers of dough. Spread a layer of dough on the table, with one corner turned towards you. Place a few vegetables in the middle. Fold the corner closest to you over the vegetables and roll halfway. Fold the left and right corners over and keep rolling to form a complete roll.

• Combine the water and flour to make a "glue". Place a little of this glue on the remaining corner of the dough and finish rolling to complete the roll. Fashion more rolls with the layers of dough and remaining vegetables.

Spicy Peanut Sauce: Combine all ingredients, taste and add Tabasco sauce as needed.

To Serve: Drop the rolls in frying oil 4 min. Drain on a paper towel. Serve with the sauce.

Checkerboard of Marinated Scallops, Cream of Red Pepper With Curry and Lime Butter

Serves 4

To create an even more colorful dish, you can replace
a few slices of scallops with marinated salmon
using the same method.

Scallops: Cut 6 scallops into 3 slices and place in a bowl. Cut the 6 other scallops into 3 slices and place in a second bowl.

Soy Marinade: Combine all ingredients required for the soy marinade. Heat 2 min. over medium heat and let cool 15 min. at room temperature. Transfer into one of the bowls with scallops. Marinate 3 hours in the refrigerator.

Sesame Oil Marinade: Roast the sesame seeds a few seconds in a frying pan. Place in a small bowl and stir in the sesame oil, lime juice and coriander. Transfer into the other bowl with scallops. Marinate 1 hour in the refrigerator.

Cream of Red Pepper: In a saucepan, melt the butter until lightly colored and sauté the onions until colored. Add the curry and apples. Sauté a few seconds and add the peppers. Add the wine, water, cream, salt and pepper. Cook 15 to 20 min. Add a little water as needed to prevent from sticking. Mix in the blender to obtain a very smooth cream. Pass through a sieve and put aside in the refrigerator.

Lime Butter: In a frying pan, sauté the shallots in butter until lightly colored. Add the lime juice and reduce by half. Add the cream and reduce by half once again. Remove from heat, add the butter and whisk vigorously to blend well. Check seasoning and put aside.

To Serve: Using a spoon, spread a little cream of red pepper on individual plates. Drain the marinated scallops and make a checkerboard over the cream of red pepper by alternating the colors. Serve the lime butter to accompany the dish. Decorate with a few lettuce shoots and rice vermicelli before serving.

INGREDIENTS

SCALLOPS
- 12 fresh scallops (10 to 20 per kg)

SOY MARINADE
- 90 g (¼ cup) molasses
- 2 tablespoons teriyaki sauce
- 1 garlic clove, crushed
- 1 lemon, quartered
- 3 star anise, ground
- 2 tablespoons orange juice

SESAME OIL MARINADE
- 1 teaspoon sesame seeds
- 60 ml (¼ cup) sesame oil
- Juice of one lime
- 1 tablespoon fresh coriander

CREAM OF RED PEPPER
- 1 tablespoon butter
- 50 g (¼ cup) onions, thinly sliced
- 1 teaspoon curry
- 1 apple, in segments
- 1 red pepper, quartered
- 60 ml (¼ cup) white wine
- 2 tablespoons water
- 2 tablespoons cream
- Salt and pepper

INGREDIENTS

LIME BUTTER

- 1 gray shallot, chopped
- 1 teaspoon butter
- 60 ml (¼ cup) lime juice
- 125 ml (½ cup) heavy cream (35 %)
- 60 g (¼ cup) unsalted butter in cubes of 1 cm (½ in.)

TO SERVE

- Lettuce shoots
- Rice vermicelli

Tuna With Marinated Ginger in a Herb Case, Beet Salad and Lime-flavored Cream

Serves 4

BEET SALAD

- 2 medium red beets, peeled and cut into 0.5 cm (¼ in.) slices
- 2 medium yellow beets, peeled and cut into 0.5 cm (¼ in.) slices
- 2 tablespoons olive oil
- Juice of one lemon
- Salt and pepper

LIME-FLAVORED CREAM

- 60 ml (¼ cup) sour cream
- 2 tablespoons heavy cream (35 %)
- 1 tablespoon lime juice
- Salt and pepper

TUNA

- 1 tablespoon marinated ginger, finely chopped
- 2 tablespoons fresh basil, chopped
- 2 tablespoons fresh coriander, chopped
- 2 tablespoons flat-leaved parsley, chopped
- 4 90 g (3 oz.) pieces of premium quality bluefin tuna
- Freshly ground salt and pepper
- 60 ml (¼ cup) olive oil
- 1 tablespoon warmed honey
- Beet shoots

The entire setup for this dish can be prepared up to two days in advance. Buy the tuna on the day of the meal, however.

Beet Salad: Cook the red and yellow beets in salted boiling water 7 to 8 min. until the tip of a knife inserted in the flesh comes easily. Cool in cold water. Combine with olive oil, lemon juice, salt and pepper and stir well. Refrigerate 1 hour to allow the olive oil to flavor the beets.

Lime-flavored Cream: Pour the sour cream and heavy cream in a bowl. Add the lime juice, salt and pepper. Stir well.

Tuna: Combine the ginger, basil, coriander and parsley on a large plate. Season the tuna well on all sides. Heat the olive oil in a non-stick pan until it smokes a little. Sear the tuna 30 seconds on all 4 sides. Remove from heat and brush the fish with warmed honey. Roll the tuna in the ginger and herb preparation and cut in two.

To Serve: Spread the lime-flavored cream on individual plates. Cover with the beet salad. Place two pieces of tuna on top and decorate with a few beet shoots before serving.

Chilean Sea Bass Marinated in Honey and Soy Sauce, Spinach and Parsnip Purée

Serves 4

The Chilean sea bass is one of my favorite fish, though it is sometimes hard to find. Remember to order it a few days ahead of time from your fish merchant. As a replacement, however, you can also use sablefish.

Fish: Bring the honey and soy sauce to a boil until the mixture is uniform. Remove from heat and let cool. Add the fish cubes and marinate for 3 hours.

Parsnip Purée: Bring the water and salt to a boil and cook the parsnips about 20 min. until the tip of a knife inserted into the flesh comes easily. Drain and mix in the food processor with the butter to obtain a smooth purée. Add salt and pepper and set aside.

Parsnip Chips: Fry slices of parsnips in oil as for fries. Drain on a paper towel and add salt.

To Serve: Drain and wipe the fish with a paper towel. Cook about 10 min. in the oven at 260°C (500°F) on the middle rack. Reduce 125 ml (½ cup) of marinade by half and set aside. Melt the butter in a frying pan. Add the spinach, salt and pepper. Stir fry 1 min. until they start to melt. Using a spoon, spread the parsnip purée on individual plates. Add the spinach in the middle, then the fish. Garnish with a few drops of marinade and parsnip chips before serving.

INGREDIENTS

FISH
- 125 ml (½ cup) honey
- 125 ml (½ cup) soy sauce
- 1 480 g (16 oz.) Chilean sea bass, cut into 4 pieces and then into evenly-sized cubes

PARSNIP PURÉE
- 1 liter (4 cups) water
- 1 teaspoon salt
- 100 g (½ cup) parsnips, peeled and diced
- 80 g (⅓ cup) unsalted butter
- Freshly ground salt and pepper

PARSNIP CHIPS
- 1 parsnip, peeled and thinly sliced
- Frying oil
- Pinch of salt

TO SERVE
- 2 tablespoons butter
- 1 liter (4 cups) miniature spinach leaves
- Freshly ground salt and pepper

Cucumber Carpaccio,
Herb and Garlic Rillettes, Salmon and
Giant Tiger Prawn Ceviche

Serves 4

INGREDIENTS

SALMON CEVICHE

- 200 g (7 oz) of salmon, cut into 12 1 x 4 cm (1/2 x 1 1/2 in.) sticks
- 75 ml (1/3 cup) olive oil
- 1 tablespoon fresh coriander, chopped
- Juice of one lime
- Salt and pepper

HERB RILLETTES

- 1 tablespoon fresh parsley, chopped
- 1 tablespoon fresh coriander, chopped
- 1 tablespoon fresh basil, chopped
- 1 tablespoon fresh chervil, chopped
- 2 tablespoons extra virgin olive oil
- 1 teaspoon butter
- 1 small garlic clove

CUCUMBER CARPACCIO

- 1 English cucumber
- 1 tablespoon olive oil
- Pinch of fleur de sel

TO SERVE

- 4 giant tiger prawns, cooked
- 60 ml (1/4 cup) mayonnaise zested with lime

PREPARATION

If you don't have a slicer handy to slice the cucumber very thin, use a peeler.

Salmon Ceviche: Place the salmon sticks in a small container. Cover with olive oil, coriander, lime juice, salt and pepper. Stir gently and set aside 1 hour in the refrigerator.

Herb Rillettes: Combine all ingredients 1 min. in the food processor and set aside in the refrigerator.

Cucumber Carpaccio: Peel the cucumber, cut it in half lengthwise and slice very thin using a slicer. Spread the cucumber slices on a plate. Brush with olive oil and season with fleur de sel.

To Serve: On individual plates, place the rillettes on the cucumbers and garnish with three pieces of salmon. Place the prawns on the rillettes and spread a little mayonnaise in a circle all around using a spoon.

Red Pepper Fondant With Espelette Pepper, Crab and Broad Bean Salad, Saffron-flavored Ailloli

Serves 4

If you don't have fresh broad beans, you can make do with frozen broad beans. Don't forget to remove the skin.

Red Pepper Fondant: Melt the butter in a saucepan. Add the onions and sweat until lightly colored. Add the peppers and sauté 5 min. over medium heat. Deglaze with white wine. Cook 2 min. and reduce to a smooth purée in the blender. Pass the mixture through a sieve to remove the particles and keep only the cream. Soften the gelatine leaves in cold water. Wring out all the water and add to the warm purée. Set aside at room temperature. Meanwhile, whip the cream until it is half whipped. Add the Espelette pepper, salt and pepper and gently stir in the purée. Spread on a 1 cm (½ in.) deep baking sheet lined with cellophane wrap. Leave at least 3 hours in the refrigerator.

Crab and Broad Bean Salad: Blanch the broad beans 3 min. in salted boiling water. Drain and cool. Remove the skin from the beans and set aside. Cook the string beans 3 min. (al dente) in salted boiling water. Cut into 5 cm (2 in.) segments. Combine the broad beans, string beans and crab meat. Cover with fresh cream, lime juice, salt and pepper. Stir well and keep in refrigerator.

Saffron-flavored Ailloli: Mix the garlic and oil in the blender to obtain a mayonnaise texture. Heat the wine and saffron lightly to release all the flavor of the spice. Let cool and add to the garlic oil. Season with salt and pepper and set aside.

To Serve: Cut the red pepper fondant into the desired shape. Place pieces of fondant in the center of individual plates and cover with salad. Garnish with a little ailloli and decorate with flower buds or fresh herbs.

INGREDIENTS

RED PEPPER FONDANT
- 1 tablespoon butter
- 30 g (¼ cup) onions, thinly sliced
- 1 red bell pepper, diced
- 2 tablespoons white wine
- 2 gelatine leaves
- 75 ml (⅓ cup) whipping cream
- Pinch of Espelette pepper
- Salt and pepper

CRAB AND BROAD BEAN SALAD
- 70 g (⅓ cup) broad beans, peeled and washed
- 8 string beans
- 100 g (¾ cup) crab meat
- 60 ml (¼ cup) fresh cream
- 1 teaspoon lime juice
- Salt and pepper

SAFFRON-FLAVORED AILLOLI
- 1 garlic clove
- 75 ml (⅓ cup) extra virgin olive oil
- 1 tablespoon white wine
- Pinch of saffron
- Salt and pepper

TO SERVE
- Flower buds
- Fresh herbs

INGREDIENTS

SCALLOPS
- 1 loaf sandwich bread
- 20 scallops
- Salt and pepper
- 60 g (⅓ cup) flour
- 2 eggs, beaten
- 80 g (⅓ cup) butter

LEMON GRANITE
- 125 ml (½ cup) water
- 1 tablespoon sugar
- Juice of one lemon

APPLE PURÉE
- 1 Golden Delicious apple, peeled and diced
- 3 tablespoons water
- 2 tablespoons extra virgin olive oil
- Salt and pepper

FRIED BASIL
- Frying oil
- 8 well-formed basil leaves
- Salt

FROTHY GARLIC MILK
- 80 ml (⅓ cup) milk
- 2 garlic cloves

PREPARATION

Keep the rest of the granite and serve between courses during another meal.

Scallops: Remove the crust from the bread and cut the soft part into small 0.5 cm (¼ in.) cubes. (You'll need 1 cup of cubes for 4 people.) Season the scallops lightly with salt and pepper. Dip the tops of the scallops in the flour, then in the beaten eggs and finally in the bread cubes. Keep on a plate in the refrigerator until ready to serve.

Lemon Granite: In a saucepan, dissolve the sugar in the water over medium heat. Remove from heat, add the lemon juice and pour onto a baking sheet. Place in the freezer until frozen.

Apple Purée: Place the apples and water in a saucepan and cook for about 10 min. over medium heat until the water has evaporated. Reduce to a purée using a food processor. Add the olive oil, salt and pepper. Add salt and pepper as needed and set aside in a small bowl.

Fried Basil: Heat the frying oil in a large saucepan or fryer. Fry the basil 30 sec. Drain on a paper towel. Salt lightly and grind.

Frothy Garlic Milk: Heat the milk and garlic about 10 min. over medium heat. Mix in the blender, filter and set aside in the refrigerator.

To Serve: Heat a saucepan over medium-high heat and add 80 g (⅓ cup) of butter. When it starts to become transparent, place the scallops with the tops down. When they start to color lightly, turn them over and cook 2 more min. Remove from heat. Remove the granite from the freezer. Using a metal spoon, scrape the ice to turn it into a very fine dust. Place this dust into small service spoons and place in the freezer until ready to serve. Spread a few strands of apple purée on individual plates. Place the hot scallops one by one. Garnish with fried basil on one side. Froth the cold milk using a small manual food processor or a milk frother. When the milk is very frothy, drop a small spoonful on each scallop. Remove the spoons containing the lemon granite from the freezer, place them on the plates and serve.

Beef Tartar, Wild Mushroom Marmelade, Truffle Oil and Bread Chips

Serves 4

Use the finest quality beef for even better results.

Marmelade: Fry the shallots 1 min. in the butter. Add the mushrooms and stir. Add the veal stock, balsamic vinegar and sugar. Reduce about 5 min. to obtain a compote. Add salt and pepper and set aside.

Bread Chips: Brush the bread slices with a little olive oil. Put them in the oven for 3 min. at 200°C (400°F) until lightly colored.

Truffle Oil: In a saucepan, bring the wine to a boil and reduce to one third of the liquid. Add the veal stock and reduce to obtain the same quantity as the reduced wine. Check seasoning. Add the truffle oil, cover and let the sauce cool down.

Tartar: In a large bowl, combine the shallots, mustard, olive oil, egg yolk, capers, parsley, truffle vinegar, Tabasco sauce, salt and pepper. Stir well using a fork to obtain a uniform paste. Add the beef tenderloin and stir well. Add Tabasco sauce, salt and pepper as needed.

To Serve: Place the tartar in the middle of a plate, glaze with the warm marmelade. Add the chips and a few shoots of mixed greens if desired. Stir the sauce gently using a spoon to avoid blending the oil with the wine sauce. Pour gently around the tartar. (The sauce and truffle oil should part and be served that way.)

INGREDIENTS

MARMELADE
- 1 gray shallot, thinly sliced
- 1 tablespoon butter
- 150 g (1 cup) mixture of 4 wild mushrooms (chanterelle, horn of plenty, hedgehog, boletus, cepe) in 1 cm (1/2 in.) pieces
- 75 ml (1/3 cup) veal stock
- 60 ml (1/4 cup) balsamic vinegar
- 1 teaspoon sugar
- Freshly ground salt and pepper

BREAD CHIPS
- 1 baguette, thinly sliced
- Extra virgin olive oil

TRUFFLE OIL SAUCE
- 60 ml (1/4 cup) red wine
- 75 ml (1/3 cup) veal stock
- Freshly ground salt and pepper
- 1 tablespoon truffle oil

TARTAR
- 1 teaspoon gray shallots, finely chopped
- 1 teaspoon hot mustard
- 1 tablespoon olive oil
- 1 egg yolk
- 16 capers, finely chopped
- 1 teaspoon fresh parsley, finely chopped
- 1 teaspoon truffle vinegar
- 5 drops Tabasco sauce
- Salt and pepper
- 200 g (7 oz.) fresh beef tenderloin, chopped with a knife
- Shoots of mixed greens (optional)

Rabbit Fondant With Benedictine Blue Cheese in a Sesame Seed Coating, Tomato Jam and Tomato Chips

Serves 4

INGREDIENTS

RABBIT FONDANT

- 1 rabbit leg
- 1 teaspoon butter
- 40 g (⅓ cup) mozzarella cheese
- 40 g (⅓ cup) Benedictine Blue Cheese from Saint-Benoît-du-Lac or other
- 2 tablespoons butter
- 2 tablespoons cream
- 2 tablespoons flour
- ½ bundle chives
- ¼ teaspoon Cajun spices
- 90 g (½ cup) flour
- 1 egg
- 125 ml (½ cup) milk
- 120 g (1 cup) sesame seeds

TOMATO JAM

- 2 tomatoes
- 1 teaspoon salt
- 1 tablespoon butter
- 50 g (¼ cup) onions, finely diced
- 75 ml (⅓ cup) balsamic vinegar
- 2 tablespoons brown sugar
- Salt and pepper
- Oil

TOMATO CHIPS

- Tomato skins
- 1 tablespoon olive oil
- Freshly ground salt and pepper
- Pinch of salt

TO SERVE

- Frying oil
- Mesclun (mixed greens)
- 1 tablespoon extra virgin olive oil
- Rice vermicelli

PREPARATION

Prepare small portions of this recipe that you can keep in the freezer and serve as hors d'oeuvres to your guests.

Rabbit Fondant: Brown the rabbit leg in butter and place in the oven for 20 min. at 180°C (350°F). Cool and cut into cubes. Cut the mozzarella and blue cheese into cubes the same size as the rabbit. Do the same with the butter and add to the mixture. Add the cream, flour, chives and Cajun spices and stir gently using a wooden spoon to avoid breaking up the pieces. Mold the preparation using an ice cream scoop or your hands to make small patties or squares depending on the desired shape. Place in the refrigerator 30 min., then roll in the flour. Combine the egg and milk and dip the cakes in the mixture. Then roll them in the sesame seeds and put aside in the refrigerator.

Tomato Jam: Make a cross incision on the tomatoes to remove the pedicel. Bring 1 liter (4 cups) of salted water to a boil and plunge the tomatoes in the water about 1 min. Remove them and put them in cold water right away. Peel off the skins using a knife and put the skins aside for later. Cut the tomatoes into small cubes. Melt the butter in a frying pan. Add the onions and tomatoes and sauté 1 min. Deglaze using the balsamic vinegar and brown sugar and cook until the tomatoes and onions break apart as in a syrupy jam. Add salt, pepper and a little oil and put aside in the refrigerator.

Tomato Chips: Brush the tomato skins with olive oil. Add salt, pepper and sugar. Place in oven 30 min. at 95°C (200°F) on a baking sheet lined with parchment paper. Check often to avoid burning.

To Serve: Fry the rabbit fondants in a deep frying pan or a small household fryer. Drop them in the oil for 6 or 7 min. depending on their size or until the inside is quite hot and the outside golden. Combine the tomato jam with the mixed greens and olive oil. Pour on the fondants and garnish with tomato chips and rice vermicelli.

Topsy-Turvy Guinea Fowl, Sweet Potatoes and Corn

Topsy-Turvy Guinea Fowl, Sweet Potatoes and Corn

Serves 4

This little exercise will show you that you can create a multitude of dishes with only a few ingredients. All you need is a little imagination!

Cream of Sweet Potato and Corn: In a saucepan, melt the butter until lightly hazelnut colored. Brown the onions 2 min. Add the sweet potatoes and corn. Sauté 2 min. and then deglaze with the stock. Cook for about 20 min. and then mix in the blender. Add the cream and put aside. Place the guinea fowl legs in a saucepan and cover with water. Cook about 30 min. until the flesh breaks apart with a fork. Drain and shred. Put aside one quarter for the cream of sweet potato and separate the rest into four equal parts for the other dishes in this recipe.

Shepherd's Pie: Preheat oven to 200°C (400°F) and cook the sweet potato 40 min. Peel and mix in the food processor with the butter to obtain a very smooth purée. Put aside in a microwave oven dish. Cook the corn 5 min. in salted boiling water. Cool right away and put aside.

Ketchup: Combine all ingredients and cook over low heat about 20 min. Put aside in the refrigerator.

Napoleon: Blanch the sweet potatoes 3 min. in boiling salted water. Drain and cool right away in cold water. Sauté in butter, add salt and pepper and put aside. Cook the corn and wine over low heat in a small saucepan and mix in blender to obtain a smooth purée. Cool in refrigerator. Meanwhile, whip the cream. Add the chives and cooled corn purée. Add salt and pepper to taste. Put aside.

Guinea Fowl Mousse and Caramel: Take a portion of meat from the guinea fowl legs and mix in food processor with the port and butter to obtain a light creamy texture. Add salt and pepper to taste. Let cool a little in the refrigerator. Meanwhile, combine the balsamic vinegar and sugar and bring to a boil to reduce by half. Put aside until ready to serve.

Corn Cakes: Combine the eggs and butter using an electric beater until uniform. Combine the flour, turmeric, corn and baking powder. Sprinkle into the eggs. Combine the ingredients gently using a spatula and pour into cupcake molds. Cook 15 to 20 min. in the oven at 180°C (350°F). Let cool and make thin slices.

INGREDIENTS

CREAM OF SWEET POTATO AND CORN
- 1 tablespoon butter
- 60 ml (¼ cup) onions, diced
- 1 sweet potato, diced
- 60 g (⅓ cup) corn niblets
- 175 ml (¾ cup) chicken stock
- 2 tablespoons heavy cream (35 %)
- 2 legs of guinea fowl

SHEPHERD'S PIE
- 1 sweet potato
- 2 tablespoons butter
- 60 g (⅓ cup) corn niblets

KETCHUP
- 30 g (¼ cup) red onions, finely shredded
- 1 tomato, diced
- 1 pear, diced
- 2 tablespoons sugar
- 2 tablespoons balsamic vinegar
- ¼ teaspoon allspice
- Salt and pepper

NAPOLEON
- 1 sweet potato, peeled and cut into 0.5 cm (¼ in.) slices
- 1 teaspoon butter
- Salt and pepper
- 45 g (¼ cup) corn niblets
- 2 tablespoons white wine
- 2 tablespoons whipping cream
- ½ teaspoon chives, chopped
- Salt and pepper

GUINEA FOWL MOUSSELINE
- 70 g (⅓ cup) guinea fowl leg meat
- 1 tablespoon port
- 60 g (¼ cup) softened butter
- Salt and pepper

CARAMEL
- 60 ml (¼ cup) balsamic vinegar
- 60 g (¼ cup) sugar

CORN CAKES
- 3 eggs
- 120 g (½ cup) softened butter
- 120 g (⅔ cup) flour
- 1 teaspoon turmeric
- 2 tablespoons corn niblets, ground
- ½ teaspoon baking powder

SWEET AND SOUR MUSTARD
- 1 tablespoon honey
- 1 tablespoon red wine vinegar
- 1 tablespoon Dijon mustard
- 1 tablespoon prepared mustard
- 60 ml (¼ cup) sweet potatoes, finely shredded
- Salt and pepper

Sweet and Sour Mustard: Combine the honey, wine vinegar, Dijon mustard and prepared mustard. Heat 2 min. in a saucepan. Remove from heat, add the sweet potatoes, salt and pepper. Let soak until ready to serve.

To Serve: Top the cake slices with a little sweet and sour mustard. Cover with lettuce leaves and a little meat from the guinea fowl legs. Make into a sandwich and cut in two.

• Heat the cream of sweet potato and pour into espresso cups. Garnish with a little meat from the guinea fowl legs.

• For the shepherd's pie, heat the sweet potato purée in the microwave oven. Sauté the corn gently in butter, then heat a little meat from the guinea fowl. Take open-ended cookie cutters and spread the hot guinea fowl meat inside. Pour a little corn on top and finish with the sweet potato purée. Remove the cutter and garnish with a small spoonful of ketchup. On another plate, alternate the sweet potato slices with small spoonfuls of guinea fowl mousseline. Finish with a little corn and whipped cream. Decorate with balsamic caramel. Place the sandwich on a plate and garnish with a small salad seasoned with a homemade dressing.

INGREDIENTS

GRAPEFRUIT CARAMEL
- 180 g (¾ cup) sugar
- 60 ml (¼ cup) water
- 2 pink grapefruits, cut into segments and skinned

TURNIP TATIN
- 4 2.5 x 10 cm (1 x 4 in.) turnip slices
- 4 12 cm (5 in.) diameter circles of puff pastry
- 4 90 g (3 oz.) slices of foie gras from Marieville or other
- Freshly ground salt and pepper
- 60 ml (¼ cup) olive oil
- 2 tablespoons grapefruit juice
- Lettuce leaves
- Fleur de sel

PREPARATION

Keep the foie gras 5 minutes in the freezer before frying it in the pan to help it keep its fat during cooking.

Grapefruit Caramel: Bring the sugar and water to a boil to obtain a clear caramel. Deglaze with the grapefruit segments. Break up the segments by stirring. Pour about 1 cm (½ in.) of this mixture in four 10 cm (4 in.) ramequins. Put aside.

Turnip Tatin: Blanch the turnips 5 min. in lightly salted boiling water. Cool in ice cold water, drain and place in the ramequins. Cover with circles of puff pastry. Place the ramequins on a baking sheet and bake in the oven at 190°C (375°F) 15 to 20 min. until the pastry is lightly colored.

To Serve: Heat a frying pan. Season the foie gras with salt and pepper and brown it in the pan on both sides. Drain on a paper towel. Turn over the ramequins on plates and gently turn them out, letting the caramel drip. Place the foie gras on top. Using a spoon, pour the rest of the caramel all around. Make a vinaigrette with the oil and grapefruit juice. Season the lettuce with salt and pepper and toss it with the vinaigrette. Garnish each plate with salad. Place a slice of foie gras on the corner with a pinch of fleur de sel.

Seared Smoked Salmon,
Frothy Hazelnut Milk, Herb Oil,
Yuzu Jelly and Chayote and Apple Salad

Serves 4

Use herb oil to replace butter if you want your mashed potatoes to stand out. Yuzu is a type of lime from Thailand whose rind is lightly dented. You can find it in Asian food markets.

Frothy Hazelnut Milk: Roast the hazelnuts 5 min. in the oven at 180°C (350°F). Let cool at room temperature and shell them by rubbing them between your hands. Combine with the milk and heat 5 min. over medium heat. Mix in the blender 2 min. and filter using a fine sieve. Let cool 15 min. in refrigerator. Add the egg white and put aside in the refrigerator.

Herb Oil: Put the oil in the blender. Add all the herbs and shred 5 min. at top speed. Put through a sieve, collect the green oil and put aside.

Yuzu Jelly: Warm the yuzu juice and combine with the softened gelatine. Pour into a small container no more than 1 cm (½ in.) deep. Let set completely about 1 hour in the refrigerator.

Chayote and Apple Salad: In a bowl, combine the chayotes, apples, oil, lemon juice, salt and pepper. Stir well.

To Serve: Take the frothy milk out of the refrigerator and froth it up 2 min. in the blender. Pour into a glass and keep in the refrigerator while you sauté the smoked salmon.

• Cut the yuzu jelly into cubes of about 1 cm (½ in.). Heat a frying pan over high heat with the hazelnut oil. Lightly season the smoked salmon with salt and pepper. Sauté over high heat about 1 min. on one side only to make it crispy underneath. Put aside on a plate.

• Make a bed of salad on individual plates. Place a piece of salmon on top. Brush the salmon with the hazelnut milk froth. Then add a few pieces of yuzu jelly. Add fresh herbs and a shot of herb oil before serving.

INGREDIENTS

FROTHY HAZELNUT MILK
- 20 g (⅔ oz.) fresh hazelnuts
- 125 ml (½ cup) milk
- 1 egg white

HERB OIL
- 75 ml (⅓ cup) sunflower oil
- 1 teaspoon chives, chopped
- 1 teaspoon flat-leaved parsley
- 1 teaspoon fresh coriander
- 1 teaspoon basil
- 1 teaspoon chervil

YUZU OR LIME JELLY
- 60 ml (¼ cup) yuzu or lime juice
- 1 leaf of gelatine, softened in cold water

CHAYOTE AND APPLE SALAD
- 1 very ripe chayote, cut into sticks
- 1 Granny Smith apple, cut into sticks
- 2 tablespoons hazelnut oil
- Juice of one lemon
- Freshly ground salt and pepper

TO SERVE
- 1 tablespoon hazelnut oil
- Slices of smoked salmon, 75 g (2½ oz.) each
- Freshly ground salt and pepper
- Remainder of fresh herbs

VEGETARIAN DISHES AND PASTA

Orzo Gratin With Beets, Aragula Pesto and Parmesan Chips

Serves 4

Orzo Gratin: Bring the water and salt to a boil. Add the orzo and cook about 8 min. (al dente). Drain in a colander and put aside. Place beets in a bowl. Bring 125 ml (½ cup) water to a boil and cook the beets about 5 min. until they are crunchy. Drain and keep the cooking water. Place the cooking water on the heat and boil until it reduces by half. Combine the beets and orzo. Add the cream, the cooking water put aside, butter, Parmesan cheese, basil, salt and pepper. Put aside in a saucepan.

Aragula Pesto: Place the pine nuts on a baking sheet and roast 5 min. in oven at 180°C (350°F). Put in the blender and add garlic, olive oil and lemon juice. Blend for 3 min. Add the aragula and blend again to obtain a smooth purée. Pour into a bowl, add salt and pepper and put aside.

Parmesan Chips: Preheat oven to 200°C (400°F). Sprinkle the Parmesan cheese sparsely on a baking sheet lined with parchment paper to form circles or triangles. Brown 8 min. in oven and put aside until ready to serve.

Garnish: Bring water and salt to a boil and cook the tomatoes and green onions 4 to 5 min. (al dente). Drain and put aside.

To Serve: Heat the orzo gratin 7 to 8 min. while stirring constantly to keep it from sticking. Sauté the tomatoes and onions in butter and season to taste. Place the orzo gratin in a bowl. Cover with the small sautéed vegetables and garnish with Parmesan chips. Pour a little aragula pesto all around and decorate with fresh herbs. Add strips of chicken for a heartier dish.

INGREDIENTS

ORZO GRATIN
- 1 liter (4 cups) water
- ¼ teaspoon salt
- 200 g (1 cup) orzo
- 150 g (2/3 cup) beets, peeled and finely shredded
- 75 ml (⅓ cup) heavy cream (35 %)
- 1 teaspoon butter
- 30 g (¼ cup) freshly grated Parmesan cheese (preferably Parmigiano Reggiano)
- 6 leaves of basil, chopped
- Salt and pepper

ARAGULA PESTO
- 1 tablespoon pine nuts
- 1 small garlic clove
- 60 ml (¼ cup) olive oil
- Lemon juice
- 1 bunch of fresh aragula, washed in icy cold water
- Freshly ground salt and pepper

PARMESAN CHIPS
- 75 ml (⅓ cup) freshly grated Parmesan cheese

GARNISH
- 500 ml (2 cups) water
- Pinch of salt
- 12 cherry tomatoes
- 12 green onions

TO SERVE
- 1 teaspoon butter
- Salt and pepper
- Fresh herbs
- Strips of chicken (optional)

Rice Patties With Shiitake Mushrooms and Marinated Ginger, Green Pepper Emulsion, Extra Virgin Olive Oil

Serves 4

INGREDIENTS

RICE PATTIES
- 250 ml (1 cup) water
- ¼ teaspoon salt
- 200 g (1 cup) basmati rice
- 3 eggs
- 60 g (⅓ cup) flour
- 2 tablespoons butter
- 12 shiitake mushrooms, finely chopped
- 1 tablespoon marinated ginger, minced
- Salt and pepper

GREEN PEPPER EMULSION
- 1 green pepper
- 1 small onion, thinly sliced
- 1 tablespoon butter
- 60 ml (¼ cup) white wine
- 60 ml (¼ cup) heavy cream (35 %)
- 60 ml (¼ cup) extra virgin olive oil

GARNISH
- 2 miniature eggplants
- 2 tablespoons olive oil
- Salt and pepper
- 75 ml (⅓ cup) milk
- 12 garlic cloves, peeled
- 1 teaspoon butter

COOKING THE PATTIES
- 1 teaspoon butter
- 1 teaspoon olive oil
- 100 g (½ cup) mushrooms
- Season vegetables (optional)
- 1 teaspoon butter

PREPARATION

Always have a good quality olive oil handy. You can prepare a simple entrée at the last minute with a few tomato slices and fresh herbs.

Rice Patties: Bring the water and salt to a boil. Add the rice and boil 5 min. Turn off the heat, cover and let sit 5 min. Transfer the rice equally into two different bowls. Cool at room temperature. Place the rice from one of the bowls in the food processor and mix with the eggs and flour about 2 min. to obtain a smooth texture. Pour into a large bowl and combine with the rice from the second bowl. Put aside. Melt the butter in a frying pan and sauté the shiitake mushrooms 3 min. over high heat. Add the ginger, then the rice, salt and pepper. Put aside.

Green Pepper Emulsion: Wrap the green pepper in foil and place in the oven 12 min. at 230°C (450°F). Remove as much skin as you can without burning yourself. Melt the butter in a frying pan and sauté the onions until lightly colored. Cut the pepper in two, empty it and place it the frying pan. Deglaze with white wine and reduce the liquid by half. Add the cream and cook 5 more min. Mix in the blender to obtain a light purée. Add a drizzle of olive oil while stirring to make an emulsion until the purée is completely uniform. Pour into a small saucepan.

Garnish: Cut the eggplants in two lengthwise and top with a drizzle of olive oil. Add salt and pepper. Bake 15 min. in the oven at 180°C (350°F). Bring the milk to a boil, add the garlic cloves and simmer 10 min. Drain, combine with the butter and brown lightly. Put aside.

Cooking the Patties: Heat the butter and olive oil in a large non-stick frying pan. Shape the rice into patties using a spoon or cutter. When the butter starts to froth, place the patties in the pan. Cook over low heat 7 to 8 min. until lightly colored. Using a large spatula, turn the patties over as for a pancake. Cook 7 to 8 more min., then put in the oven 5 min. at 180°C (350°F). Meanwhile, heat the green pepper emulsion lightly. Sauté the eggplants, mushrooms and season vegetables in butter.

To Serve: Place the patties in the middle of the plates, garnish with the green pepper emulsion and the other vegetables.

Tortiglioni With Snails, Sun-dried Tomatoes, Herbs and Garlic

Serves 4

In a large saucepan, bring the water and salt to a boil. Add the tortiglioni and cook 8 min. (al dente). Drain and put aside. Pour the olive oil into a large saucepan over high heat. Add the snails, sun-dried tomatoes, herbs and garlic. Sauté 1 min. over high heat. Add salt and pepper. Combine with the warm pasta, check seasoning and sauté 1 min. Serve in bowls.

INGREDIENTS

- 2 liters (8 cups) water
- 2 teaspoons salt
- 1 package of tortiglioni
- 75 ml (1/3 cup) extra virgin olive oil
- 32 snails
- 45 g (1/4 cup) sun-dried tomatoes, chopped
- 1 tablespoon chives
- 1 tablespoon parsley
- 1 tablespoon basil
- 1 garlic clove
- Freshly ground salt and pepper

FISH AND SEAFOOD DISHES

Fillet of Arctic Char With a Black Olive Coating, Virgin Sauce and Ratte Potato and Fennel Fricassée

Serves 4

**This dish is also exquisite served cold as a salad meal.
Round carrots are a miniature carrot variety.**

Black Olive Coating: Mix the olives and olive oil 1 min. in the blender to obtain a smooth texture. Transfer into a bowl, add the breadcrumbs and Parmesan cheese and stir with a wooden spoon. Add the thyme and capers. Put aside in the refrigerator.

Virgin Sauce: Put the olive oil in a small saucepan. Heat lightly, add the onions and sauté until they are transparent. Add the tomatoes and remove from heat immediately. Add the dill, basil, Pernod, salt, pepper and lemon juice. Stir and put aside.

Potato Fricassée: Cut the potatoes into 0.5 cm (¼ in.) slices. Heat the butter in a saucepan. When it starts to froth, add the potatoes and fennel. Sauté 8 min. over high heat while stirring to keep the mixture from sticking. Deglaze with white wine and reduce by half. Add the cream and cook 5 min. Remove from heat. Add the dill, salt and pepper. Put aside.

Garnish: Cook the carrots in salted boiling water about 8 min. (al dente). Sauté in butter. Add salt and pepper. Put aside.

Fish: Season the fish with salt and pepper. Spread a little black olive crust on the fillets. Heat the olive oil in a frying pan and place the fillets on top using a spatula with the olive coating on top. Sauté 3 min. over medium heat without turning them over. Add the carrots to warm them up and finish cooking in the oven for 2 min. at 200°C (400°F) so that the black olives become lightly crusted.

To Serve: Warm the virgin sauce in the microwave oven or in a pan. Place the warm potato fricassée in a bowl or plate. Cover with the fish, garnish with a little virgin sauce all around and decorate with the carrots.

INGREDIENTS

BLACK OLIVE COATING
- 20 Kalamata olives, pitted
- 60 ml (¼ cup) extra virgin olive oil
- 1 tablespoon breadcrumbs
- 1 tablespoon Parmesan cheese
- 1 teaspoon fresh thyme, chopped
- 12 capers, finely chopped

VIRGIN SAUCE
- 125 ml (½ cup) extra virgin olive oil
- 2 tablespoons onions, finely chopped
- 1 tomato, diced
- 1 tablespoon fresh dill, chopped
- 1 tablespoon fresh basil, chopped
- 1 teaspoon Pernod
- Freshly ground salt and pepper
- 2 tablespoons lemon juice

POTATO FRICASSÉE
- 360 g (12 oz.) ratte potatoes, washed
- 60 g (¼ cup) butter
- 1 bulb of fennel, cut into 1 cm (½ in.) cubes
- 125 ml (½ cup) white wine
- 200 ml (¾ cup + 1 tablespoon) heavy cream (35 %)
- 1 teaspoon fresh dill, chopped
- Freshly ground salt and pepper

GARNISH
- 12 round or regular carrots
- 1 teaspoon butter
- Salt and pepper

FISH
- 4 150 g (5 oz.) fillets of Arctic Char, skinned
- Freshly ground salt and pepper
- 1 tablespoon olive oil

INGREDIENTS

PREPARATION

- 1 tablespoon butter
- Gray shallots
- 60 ml (¼ cup) white wine
- 425 ml (1¾ cup) fish stock
- 2 tablespoons flour
- 125 ml (½ cup) heavy cream (35 %)
- 60 ml (¼ cup) violet mustard
- 100 g (3½ oz.) carrots, cut into sticks
- 100 g (3½ oz.) baby string beans
- 100 g (3½ oz.) small round potatoes
- 90 g (3 oz.) fennel, diced
- 100 g (3½ oz.) sweet peas
- 720 g (1½ lbs) Atlantic salmon, in 2 cm (1 in.) cubes
- 2 tablespoons fresh mint, chopped

When friends come over, serve the stew in a soup tureen that you can set on the table so that everyone can serve him or herself.

• Sweat the shallots in butter. Add the wine and reduce by half. Add the fish stock. Bring to a boil and reduce by three quarters. Whisk the flour in the cream and pour onto the broth while whisking vigorously. Cook 10 min. and then add the mustard.

• Meanwhile, blanch the vegetables in salted water 5 min. Cool and put aside. Drop the salmon cubes into the sauce with the vegetables and mint. Simmer 5 min. and serve.

Brandade With Blue Potatoes in a Poor Man's Pastry, Creamy Pernod Sauce With Mushrooms

Serves 4

If you don't have baguette, flatten a few slices of ordinary bread with a rolling pin.

Brandade: Place the cod fillets in a large saucepan with the wine and cream. Cook about 8 min. until they break apart easily. Put aside. Cook the potatoes in salted water. When the tip of a knife inserted into the flesh comes easily, drain and mash. Add the cod and butter. Stir well using a wooden spoon. Salt as needed and add the dill.

Creamy Pernod Sauce with Mushrooms: Combine the shallots and mushrooms. Melt the butter in a saucepan until it starts to froth. Thoroughly sauté the shallots and mushrooms. Deglaze with the white wine and then the Pernod. Add the fish stock and reduce by half. Add the cream and simmer 5 min. Put aside.

Croutons: Cut the baguette diagonally into thin slices as long as you can make them (you'll need 3 slices per person). Brush with olive oil and brown 5 min. in the oven preheated to 200°C (400°F). Put aside.

Vegetables with Aragula Pesto: Blanch the string beans in salted water and cool them right away with ice water. Put aside in a container. Blanch the turnips in salted water for about 8 min. Cool in ice water and put aside with the string beans. Heat a frying pan and sauté the onions 3 min. in butter. Add the string beans and the turnips and sauté a few seconds. Add the pesto, salt and pepper and stir well.

To Serve: If the brandade is not very warm, heat it up a few seconds in the microwave oven. Do the same for the cream of Pernod and the vegetables. In a large plate, shape the brandade purée into quenelles using two big spoons. Take a little purée with a spoon and, using the other spoon, take the purée and bring it towards you while carefully scraping the inside of the spoon. Wash the spoons and start over. Make three quenelles per plate and place the croutons between them. Top with a little cream of Pernod with mushrooms and add the vegetables as an accompaniment.

INGREDIENTS

BRANDADE
- 600 g (20 oz.) fresh cod fillets (carefully remove all the bones)
- 60 ml (¼ cup) white wine
- 125 ml (½ cup) cream
- 480 g (1 lb) blue potatoes, peeled
- 1 liter (4 cups) water
- Pinch of salt
- 60 g (¼ cup) butter
- 1 tablespoon fresh dill, finely chopped

CREAMY PERNOD SAUCE WITH MUSHROOMS
- 2 gray shallots, thinly sliced
- 150 g (1 cup) mushrooms, sliced
- 1 tablespoon butter
- 75 ml (⅓ cup) white wine
- 1 tablespoon Pernod
- 125 ml (½ cup) fish stock
- 60 ml (¼ cup) cream

CROUTONS
- 1 baguette
- Extra virgin olive oil

VEGETABLES WITH ARAGULA PESTO
- 24 fine baby string beans, trimmed
- 6 turnips, cut into sticks
- 1 onion, in slices of 0.5 cm (¼ in.)
- 1 tablespoon butter
- 2 tablespoons aragula pesto (p. 62)
- Freshly ground salt and pepper

INGREDIENTS

PARSNIP MILK
- 1 teaspoon butter
- 30 g (¼ cup) onions, thinly sliced
- 2 parsnips, peeled and sliced into rounds
- 125 ml (½ cup) chicken stock
- Salt and pepper
- 75 ml (⅓ cup) milk
- 60 ml (¼ cup) cream

CANDIED SHALLOTS
- 20 gray shallots
- 1 teaspoon butter
- Salt and pepper
- 1 tablespoon basil, chopped

CREAMY POLENTA
- 125 ml (½ cup) milk
- 2 tablespoons butter
- 45 g (¼ cup) corn flour
- 100 g (3⅓ oz.) 'Victor et Berthold' cheese or other semi-firm cheese

TOMATO MELT
- 1 fresh tomato
- 1 tablespoon olive oil
- 1 tablespoon onions, finely shredded
- 60 ml (¼ cup) white wine
- 1 tablespoon tomato paste
- 1 teaspoon sugar
- 1 drop Tabasco sauce
- Salt and pepper
- 1 tablespoon pine nuts

FISH
- 4 150 g (5 oz.) pollack steaks
- Freshly ground salt and pepper

Pollack Steak Poached in Parsnip Milk, Candied Shallots and Creamy Polenta With 'Victor et Berthold' Cheese

Serves 4

PREPARATION

Using a spoon, take the time to baste the fish with the parsnip milk during cooking. This will make the dish even tastier.

Parsnip Milk: Melt the butter in a saucepan. Add the onions and parsnips. Sauté until lightly colored. Deglaze with the chicken stock and cook 20 min. Mix in the blender to obtain a broth. Add salt and pepper. Put back in the saucepan. Add the milk and cream and put aside.

Candied Shallots: Preheat the oven to 180°C (350°F). Spread the shallots on a baking sheet and cook 45 min. Let cool at room temperature. When they are warm, press firmly on the bulb (near the root) to strip them. Combine with the butter, salt, pepper and basil. Put aside.

Creamy Polenta: Bring the milk to a boil in a saucepan. Add the butter and corn flour. Using a whisk, stir vigorously to avoid forming lumps. Add the cheese and stir 2 to 3 min. using a wooden spoon. Cover and put aside.

Tomato Melt: Remove the pedicel on the tomato and make a cross-shaped incision on the bottom part without going too deep into the flesh. Plunge the tomato in salted boiling water about 30 sec. Cool immediately in ice water. Peel the tomato, cut it in four and remove the seeds and juice. Dice the flesh and put aside in a small bowl. In a saucepan, sweat the onions in olive oil. Add the diced tomatoes and the wine. Add the tomato paste, sugar and Tabasco sauce. Simmer over medium heat 8 to 10 min. until the liquid has completely evaporated. Add salt and pepper to taste. Roast the pine nuts 5 min. at 180°C (350°F) and add them to the tomato melt.

Fish: Place the fish in a deep saucepan. Cover with the parsnip milk and cook about 12 min. in the oven preheated to 180°C (350°F).

To Serve: Reheat the candied shallots. Make sure the polenta and tomato melt are hot. Place the pollack on a plate, top with the parsnip milk. Add a stroke of creamy polenta on the side, garnish with the candied shallots and put a little tomato melt on top.

Striped Bass in the Pan,
Creamy Fingerling Potatoes,
Aniseed Spinach With Turmeric Broth

Serves 4

Ask your fish merchant to prepare the fillets for you.
Season the fish only once it has seared. This will prevent it
from sticking to the pan. You can easily find turmeric
roots in Asian grocery stores.

Creamy Potatoes: Bring the water and salt to a boil in a saucepan. Add the potatoes and cook 15 min. Drain and place in a bowl. Using a big fork, grind them to obtain a chunky purée. Add the cream, butter, salt and pepper and stir well. Add the chives and put aside.

Turmeric Broth: In a saucepan, melt the butter and sauté the shallots 2 min. until lightly colored. Add the turmeric roots and sauté 1 min. Add the wine and reduce by half. Add the fish stock and reduce by half. Add the cream and mix all ingredients in the blender 2 min. at high speed. Pass through a sieve, add salt and pepper as needed and keep warm.

Garnish: In a saucepan, combine the fennel, orange juice, saffron, 1 tablespoon butter, salt and pepper. Cook 5 min. and put aside. Melt the remaining butter in another pan. Add the spinach and sauté a few moments until they start to melt. Add the Pernod, salt and pepper. Stir and keep warm.

Fish: Season the fillets with salt and pepper. Heat a pan over high heat with olive oil. When the oil starts fuming, cook the fish 2 min. on one side and then 1 min. on the other. Remove the pan from the heat.

To Serve: Pour the creamy potatoes into a bowl. Cover with the spinach. Place the heated fillets. Top with the turmeric broth and garnish with the fennel.

INGREDIENTS

CREAMY POTATOES
- 500 ml (2 cups) water
- Pinch of salt
- 240 g (8 oz.) Fingerling potatoes
- 250 ml (1 cup) cream
- 80 g (⅓ cup) butter
- Freshly ground salt and pepper
- 1 tablespoon fresh chives, chopped

TURMERIC BROTH
- 1 tablespoon butter
- 2 gray shallots
- 2 turmeric roots, peeled and thinly sliced
- 75 ml (⅓ cup) white wine
- 125 ml (½ cup) fish stock
- 60 ml (¼ cup) cream
- Salt and pepper

GARNISH
- 1 fennel, peeled and cut into sticks
- 2 tablespoons orange juice
- 1 pinch saffron
- 2 teaspoons butter
- Salt and pepper
- 500 ml (2 cups) spinach
- 1 teaspoon Pernod

FISH
- 2 striped bass of 480 g (1 lb.) each, cut into fillets with bones and skin removed
- Salt and pepper
- 1 tablespoon olive oil

Lobster Tail Casserole With Steamed Basil, Lobster Claw Lasagna, Curried Coconut Milk

Lobster Tail Casserole With Steamed Basil, Lobster Claw Lasagna, Curried Coconut Milk

Serves 4

The recipe for red curry sauce is similar to Thai curry dishes. Make a bigger batch that you can use for other meals with chicken, mussels or shrimp.

Lobster Tail Casserole: Cook the lobsters 6 min. in boiling water. Let cool. Remove the shell, taking care to keep it in one piece.

Lasagna: Cook the pasta 7 min. in salted boiling water. Drain. Add a drizzle of olive oil and let cool in the refrigerator. Heat the olive oil in a saucepan and sauté the bell peppers, shallots and onions 2 min., stirring from time to time to prevent them from coloring. Add the pineapple and put aside in a bowl.

Curried Coconut Milk: Combine the citronella, garlic and curry paste. In a saucepan, heat the vegetable oil and sauté this mixture 2 min. over medium heat. Add the lime leaves and stir a few seconds using a wooden spatula. Add the coconut milk. Bring to a boil. Add the fish sauce and brown sugar. Simmer 15 min. over low heat. Pass through a sieve and keep only the sauce.

Curried Whipped Cream: Whip the cream to three-quarters stiffness and add the curry. Whip until peaks form and put aside.

To Serve: Heat 125 ml (½ cup) curried coconut milk in a frying pan. Add the lobster tails, mushrooms and basil. Warm 2 min. and pour into small individual casseroles. In a frying pan, heat the butter until hazelnut colored. Using a spoon, top the lobster tails with the melted butter. Cover the casseroles and keep warm in the oven at 95°C (200°F) while preparing to serve the meal.

• Deglaze the sautéed vegetables with the remaining coconut milk and heat 5 min. Melt a knob of butter, add the lobster claws, season well and sauté 1 min. on each side. On each individual plate, place a spoonful of vegetables, cover with a strip of lasagna pasta and repeat. Do the same with other vegetables and another strip of pasta and finish with 2 lobster claws. Take the leftover butter from the pan using a spoon to top the lasagna. Place a small spoonful of curried whipped cream on each lasagna dish, put the casserole on the plate and serve.

INGREDIENTS

LOBSTER TAIL CASSEROLE
- 4 lobsters of 480 to 720 g (1 to 1½ lb.) each
- 75 g (½ cup) mushrooms, thinly sliced
- 125 ml (½ cup) Thai basil
- 1 tablespoon butter

LASAGNA
- 8 15 cm (6 in.) sheets of lasagna, fresh if possible
- 1 tablespoon olive oil
- 1 red pepper, cut into 1 cm (½ in.) cubes
- 1 green pepper, cut into 1 cm (½ in.) cubes
- 1 yellow pepper, cut into 1 cm (½ in.) cubes
- 1 green onion, cut into 1 cm (½ in.) cubes
- 1 small red onion, cut into 1 cm (½ in.) cubes
- 60 ml (¼ cup) pineapple, diced
- 8 lobster claws

CURRIED COCONUT MILK
- 1 stick of citronella, thinly sliced
- 1 garlic clove, thinly sliced
- 1 tablespoon red curry paste
- 1 tablespoon vegetable oil
- 4 leaves of lime
- 1 can coconut milk
- 1 teaspoon fish sauce
- 1 teaspoon brown sugar

CURRIED WHIPPED CREAM
- 60 ml (¼ cup) whipping cream
- 1 teaspoon red curry

INGREDIENTS

FISH AND CHIPS

- 2 Idaho potatoes, peeled and cut into 36 thin slices lengthwise
- Salt and pepper
- 4 monkfish fillets of 180 g (6 oz.) each, 10 cm (4 in.) wide
- Butter

OLIVE POWDER

- 10 Kalamata olives, pitted

CREAM OF TOMATO

- 1 teaspoon butter
- ½ onion, thinly sliced
- 3 tomatoes, quartered
- 75 ml (⅓ cup) white wine
- 125 ml (½ cup) chicken stock
- 75 ml (⅓ cup) extra virgin olive oil
- Freshly ground salt and pepper

GARNISH

- Savoy cabbage, very thinly sliced
- White wine
- Freshly ground salt and pepper

PREPARATION

This recipe is best prepared at least 6 hours in advance.

Fish and Chips: Spread a cellophane wrap over your work area. Place 9 potato slices so that they overlap (3 vertical slices x 3 horizontal slices). Season generously with salt and pepper. Place a fish fillet on top. Roll using the plastic wrap. Do the same to make three other fish and chip packages. Put aside 30 min. in the refrigerator.

Olive Powder: Dry the olives 4 hours in the oven at 80°C (175°F). Reduce to a fine powder using a food processor and put aside.

Cream of Tomato: In a saucepan, melt the butter over medium-high heat. Sauté the onions and tomatoes. Deglaze with the white wine and chicken stock. Cook 20 min., then mix in the blender 2 min. to obtain a smooth creamy texture. While the blender is spinning, slowly add the olive oil to make the sauce creamier. Add salt and pepper as needed and put aside.

Garnish: In a saucepan, cook the cabbage in white wine about 20 min. over medium heat. Add salt and pepper as needed. Heat a non-stick pan over high heat. Add the butter and heat it until it becomes frothy. Carefully remove the wrap from the fish and chips. Add salt and pepper on the outside surface of the fish and chips. Place them in the pan. Brown them gently until they are colored. Turn them over often. Finish cooking them in the oven at 190°C (375°F).

To Serve: Meanwhile, place the cabbage on individual plates. Pour a little cream of tomato on top and place a piece of fish in the middle. Garnish with olive powder and serve.

Hearty Seafood Soup, Spicy Broth and Marinated Vegetable Rouelles

Serves 4

Marinate the vegetables the day before to give them more taste.

Marinated Vegetable Rouelles: Combine the onions, carrots, peppers, snow peas and mango. Stir in the rice vinegar, sesame oil, canola oil, garlic and miso. Add salt and pepper. Put in the refrigerator about 30 min. Thoroughly drain the marinade. Spread the Chinese cabbage leaves and cut them in two lengthwise. Place a few vegetables in the middle and make into rolls (three per person). Place the rolls on a plate.

Seafood Soup: Bring the stock to a boil and gently drop in the mussels and clams. Cook 2 min. Add the scallops, shrimp and squid. Cook another min. and turn off the heat.

To Serve: Put the vermicelli into large bowls and add a little coriander. Using a ladle, add the broth and seafood. Serve with the marinated vegetable rolls.

INGREDIENTS

MARINATED VEGETABLE ROLLS

- 1 red onion, thinly sliced
- 1 carrot, cut into sticks
- 2 yellow peppers, cut into sticks
- 12 snow peas, cut into sticks
- 1 mango, cut into sticks
- 1 tablespoon rice vinegar
- 2 tablespoons sesame oil
- 60 ml (¼ cup) canola oil
- 1 small garlic clove, chopped
- 1 tablespoon miso
- Salt and pepper
- Chinese cabbage leaves

SEAFOOD SOUP

- Spicy vegetable broth (p. 18)
- 20 mussels, scrubbed to remove the beards
- 12 hard-shell clams, washed
- 12 scallops
- 16 shrimp, shelled and deveined
- 2 squid, washed and cut into thin slices
- 1 package rice vermicelli, soaked 30 min in cold water
- 1 bunch fresh coriander, leaves removed and thoroughly washed

Poached Foie Gras With Veal and Soy Broth, Sautéed Shrimp and Ginger Chow Mein

Serves 4

VEAL AND SOY BROTH

- 1 liter (4 cups) veal stock
- 125 ml (½ cup) cream
- 60 ml (¼ cup) soy sauce

GINGER CHOW MEIN

- 250 ml (1 cup) Chinese cabbage, thinly sliced
- 1 small onion, thinly sliced
- 100 g (½ cup) carrots, thinly sliced into rounds
- 1 green onion, chopped
- 60 g (½ cup) soy bean sprouts
- 1 stalk celery, very thinly sliced diagonally
- Vegetable oil
- 1 tablespoon freshly grated ginger
- Freshly ground salt and pepper

SHRIMP

- 8 jumbo shrimp (10 to 12 per kg)
- 1 tablespoon butter
- Olive oil
- Freshly ground salt and pepper

FOIE GRAS

- 400 g (13 oz.) fresh premium quality foie gras, cut into 4 slices
- Freshly ground pepper

Take care to select premium quality foie gras to avoid the unpleasant taste of veins.

Veal and Soy Broth: Bring the veal stock to a boil in a saucepan and reduce to 250 ml (1 cup). Add the cream and soy sauce and simmer 2 min. Put aside in a large saucepan that can contain the slices of foie gras.

Ginger Chow Mein: Combine the Chinese cabbage, onions, carrots, green onions, soy bean sprouts and celery.

To Serve: Heat a wok-type pan and another pan for the shrimp. Pour the vegetable oil into the wok. Add the ginger and the vegetables. Sauté 3 min. over high heat. Add salt and pepper to taste. Melt the butter with a little oil in the second pan. Add salt and pepper to the shrimp and sauté 4 min. over high heat. Let the veal broth simmer and cook the foie gras 2 min. Turn over using a spatula and cook another min. Turn off the heat.

To Serve: Put the chow mein into deep bowls and cover with the foie gras. Pour the sauce onto plates, place the shrimp on top and serve.

Hot and Cold Lobster

Serves 4

This recipe may seem a little long to prepare,
but with a little organization and preparation,
it's well worth the time.

Avocado Ice: Peel and pit the avocado. Cut into quarters and place in a
bowl. In a saucepan, bring the cream, glucose, lemon juice and a little salt
and pepper to a boil. Pour into a bowl containing the egg yolk. Stir
immediately with a whisk until uniform and put back on the heat 30 sec.
Remove from heat and combine with the avocado. Mix in the blender at
high speed to obtain a very smooth texture. Pass through a China cap
strainer and keep 3 hours in the freezer. To finish the avocado ice, mix it
in the food processor 1 min. to obtain a smooth creamy texture and put it
back in the freezer 30 min. before serving to let it cool.

White Bisque: Heat a deep saucepan over high heat. Add the canola oil.
When it starts to heat, add the lobster shells and sauté with the onions.
Deglaze with white wine, and then cognac. Add the fish stock and simmer
about 20 min. Pass through a China cap strainer and reduce by half over
high heat. Add the cream, salt and pepper. Keep warm.

Whipped Turmeric Cream: Whip the cream and add the turmeric. Put aside in
the refrigerator.

Lobster: Roll the lobster tails in the flour, and then in the tempura batter.
Drain thoroughly and drop into the fryer until the batter is crunchy.
Remove from the oil and drain on a paper towel.
Season and put aside until ready to serve.

Truffle Oil Mayonnaise: Put a little water in a saucepan over high heat. In a
bowl that will fit over the saucepan, put the egg yolks and mustard. Whisk
briskly to prevent the yolks from cooking. Add a fine trickle of truffle oil
and grape seed oil. When the texture thickens to that of a mayonnaise,
remove from heat. Add salt, pepper and lemon juice. Put aside.

To Serve: Pour the bisque into small heated espresso cups. Add a spoonful
of whipped turmeric cream and a little warm mayonnaise in the middle of
the plate. Garnish with five slices of cucumber placed in a circle. Put the
fried lobster tail on top and garnish with a small quenelle of avocado ice.

INGREDIENTS

AVOCADO ICE
- 1 ripe avocado
- 75 ml (⅓ cup) cream
- 1 teaspoon glucose
- Juice of one lemon
- Salt and pepper
- 1 egg yolk

WHITE BISQUE
- 1 tablespoon canola oil
- 2 lobster shells
- 1 onion, thinly sliced
- 125 ml (½ cup) white wine
- 1 tablespoon cognac
- 250 ml (1 cup) fish stock
- 75 ml (⅓ cup) cream
- Salt and pepper

WHIPPED TURMERIC CREAM
- 60 ml (¼ cup) whipping cream
- 1/2 teaspoon turmeric powder
- 4 lobster claws

LOBSTER
- 2 lobster tails, cut in two lengthwise
- Flour
- Tempura batter, sold in supermarkets
- Frying oil
- Salt
- 1 cucumber, thinly sliced

TRUFFLE OIL MAYONNAISE
- 2 egg yolks
- 1 teaspoon Dijon mustard
- 2 tablespoons truffle oil
- 60 ml (¼ cup) grape seed oil
- Salt and pepper
- ½ teaspoon lemon juice

86   FISH AND SEAFOOD DISHES

RESTAURANT

CHEZ L'ÉPICIER

Nº311

ST-PAUL EST
MTL

ET BAR À VIN

Risotto With Duck Leg Confit, Fried Onions, Sherry Vinegar Juice and Truffle Honey Glazed Carrots

Serves 4

INGREDIENTS

RISOTTO
- 80 g (⅓ cup) butter
- 50 g (¼ cup) onions, chopped
- 1 garlic clove, chopped
- 300 g (1½ cups) arborio rice
- 250 ml (1 cup) white wine
- 750 ml (3 cups) chicken stock
- 150 g (¾ cup) chanterelles, thoroughly washed and quartered
- 3 duck legs confit, shredded
- 3 tablespoons fresh parsley, finely chopped
- 75 ml (⅓ cup) cream
- 80 g (⅓ cup) butter
- 30 g (¼ cup) Parmesan cheese
- Salt and pepper

OLD SHERRY VINEGAR JUICE
- 1 teaspoon butter
- 2 gray shallots, chopped
- 125 ml (½ cup) old sherry vinegar, at least 15 years old if possible
- 1 teaspoon sugar
- 250 ml (1 cup) brown veal stock
- Salt and pepper
- 1 teaspoon butter

TRUFFLE HONEY GLAZED CARROTS
- 12 miniature carrots, peeled
- 1 tablespoon truffle honey or regular honey
- 1 tablespoon butter
- Freshly ground salt and pepper

FRIED ONIONS
- 1 white onion, cut into rings
- 45 g (¼ cup) flour
- 1 tablespoon butter
- Salt

PREPARATION

If you don't have time to prepare the duck legs, you can find them in supermarkets.

Risotto: Melt the butter in a saucepan. Add the onions and garlic and gently sauté until they start to become transparent. Add the rice and continue sautéing in butter until it gleams a little. Add one quarter of the white wine and one quarter of the stock. Stir often to prevent the rice from sticking and simmer gently for 5 min. Add one quarter of the wine and stock and cook 5 min., stirring constantly. Repeat these steps twice until no wine or stock remains. Don't forget to stir often. When the rice is cooked, put aside.

Old Sherry Vinegar Juice: Melt the butter in a saucepan and sauté the shallots until they start to brown. Deglaze with old sherry vinegar. Add the sugar and reduce by half. Add the brown veal stock and reduce again by half. Add salt, pepper and the butter. Stir and put aside. (If you prefer a thicker sauce, it can be thickened.)

Truffle Honey Glazed Carrots: Place the carrots in a small saucepan and cover with salted water. Cook 5 min. over high heat. Add the honey, butter, salt and pepper. Cook 2 more min. Check if they are done by inserting the tip of a knife. It should come easily. Remove from heat and put aside.

Final Steps: Combine the rice and the chanterelles, the duck legs, parsley, cream, butter and Parmesan cheese. Heat 7 to 8 min. over medium heat. Add salt and pepper as needed. Meanwhile, roll the onions in flour. In a frying pan, melt the butter. Sauté the onions until they are lightly colored. Add a little salt, place on a paper towel to remove excess fat and put aside. Heat the glazed carrots and sherry vinegar juice a few seconds.

To Serve: Shape the risotto using a ramequin, funnel or any other mold according to the desired shape. Put in the middle of the plate. Pour a little sherry vinegar juice, garnish with glazed carrots and finish with the fried onions.

Guinea Fowl Supremes Stuffed With Mangos, Hot Mustard and Green Cabbage, Creamy Bacon Sauce

Serves 4

You don't like cabbage? I insist that you try this dish. Let me know what you think...

Mango and Cabbage Compote: Combine the mango and cabbage. Put in a saucepan over medium-high heat with the wine, mustard, salt and pepper. Cook until it starts to boil, lower the heat to medium and cook about 10 min. until the texture is that of a compote. Transfer the mixture into a bowl and let cool at room temperature.

Guinea Fowl: Preheat oven to 190°C (375°F). Meanwhile, using a spoon, make an incision on the back part of the supremes (near the bone). Open the breasts three quarters of the way. Stuff with the compote. Melt the butter in a frying pan over medium heat until hazelnut colored. Add salt and pepper to the supremes on both sides. Fry them quickly in the pan 2 min. on each side. Place on a baking sheet and cook 12 min. in the oven.

Creamy Bacon Sauce: Melt the butter in a saucepan. Add the shallots and sauté gently. Add the bacon and cook until lightly colored. Deglaze with the white wine. Reduce by half, add the cream and simmer 2 min. Mix in the blender at high speed to obtain a creamy texture. Pass through a sieve and keep warm.

Garnish: Place the radishes in a small pan with the water, sugar, butter, salt and pepper. Cover and cook 7 to 8 min. until the water has evaporated and the radishes are cooked. Heat a frying pan and sauté the brussels sprouts about 30 sec. with the water and butter.

To Serve: Spread the bacon sauce on individual plates. Place a few radishes in the middle and a few brussels sprout leaves all around. Cut a supreme in two, place in the middle and serve.

MANGO AND CABBAGE COMPOTE
- 1 very ripe mango, peeled and cut into 2 cm (1 in.) cubes
- 400 g (2 cups) savoy cabbage, trimmed and cut into cubes
- 75 ml (⅓ cup) white wine
- 60 ml (¼ cup) Dijon mustard
- Freshly ground salt and pepper

GUINEA FOWL
- 4 guinea fowl supremes
- 1 tablespoon butter
- Freshly ground salt and pepper

CREAMY BACON SAUCE
- 1 teaspoon butter
- 2 gray shallots, chopped
- 60 g (⅓ cup) bacon, diced
- 125 ml (½ cup) white wine
- 125 ml (½ cup) cream

GARNISH
- 36 radishes of various types, thoroughly washed
- 125 ml (½ cup) water
- 80 g (⅓ cup) sugar
- 60 g (¼ cup) butter
- Salt and pepper
- 16 brussels sprouts, leaves loosened
- Water
- Butter

Roasted Duck Breasts, Poached Rhubarb With Aniseed and Parsnip Darphins With Thai Basil

Serves 4

INGREDIENTS

DUCK
- 2 whole ducks without the legs
- Salt and pepper to taste

POACHED RHUBARB
- 500 ml (2 cups) water
- 180 g (³/₄ cup) sugar
- 1 tablespoon aniseed
- 4 stalks fresh rhubarb, peeled and cut into 8 cm (3 in.) sticks

PARSNIP DARPHINS
- 3 parsnip roots, finely grated
- 2 eggs
- 60 ml (¹/₄ cup) heavy cream (35 %)
- 1 sprig of Thai basil
- Salt and pepper to taste
- 2 tablespoons butter

SAUCE
- 1 tablespoon butter
- 1 teaspoon aniseed
- 125 ml (¹/₂ cup) port
- 250 ml (1 cup) veal stock
- Salt and pepper

GARNISH
- 200 g (1 cup) broad beans, shelled
- 1 tablespoon butter
- Salt and pepper

PREPARATION

If you can't find Thai basil, you can replace it with ordinary basil and a pinch of cinnamon.

Duck: Season the entire ducks with salt and pepper and keep them in the refrigerator until ready to cook. Preheat oven to 200°C (400°F) and cook the ducks 8 min. Lower the temperature to 180°C (350°F) and cook 7 more min.

Poached Rhubarb: Bring the water, sugar and aniseed to a boil in a saucepan. When it starts to boil, poach the rhubarb until the tip of a knife inserted into the flesh comes easily. Remove from the saucepan and put aside.

Parsnip Darphins: Combine all the ingredients except the butter. Make patties out of this mixture. In a non-stick saucepan, melt the butter over medium-high heat. When it starts to froth, gently deposit the darphins using a spatula. Fry 3 min. until they start to brown. Turn over the patties. Place them on a baking sheet and put them in the oven 10 min. at 200°C (400°F). Put aside.

Sauce: In a saucepan, melt the butter over medium heat until hazelnut colored. Add the aniseed and sauté a few seconds. Deglaze with port and reduce by half. Add the veal stock and reduce once again. Add salt and pepper as needed and keep warm.

Garnish: Sauté the broad beans in butter. Add salt and pepper and put aside.

To Serve: Take the ducks out of the oven. Lift out the breasts by separating the chest with a pointed knife. Pry the breasts off the bone. Cut into three pieces. Reheat the rhubarb as needed and place it on the plate. Place the duck cutlets on top and garnish with a little sauce. Cut the darphins in two and place them on the plate with a spoonful of warm broad beans.

Québec Lamb Tatin With Caramelized Endives, Cauliflower Purée With Goat Milk Cheese and Black Olive Emulsion

Serves 4

To lower the fat content of this recipe, braise the lamb in lamb stock rather than duck fat.

Lamb Tatin: Preheat oven to 120°C (250°F). Place the lamb shoulder and the duck fat in an oven-proof saucepan. Cover and cook 4 hours in the oven. Meanwhile, sauté the onions in butter until they caramelize. Put aside. When the lamb is ready, take it out of the oven and check if it breaks apart easily with a fork. Remove it from the duck fat and drain it 5 min. to remove all the fat. While still hot, put the lamb in a bowl, add the onions and stir vigorously with a wooden spoon until everything is shredded and blends well. Add the olive oil, salt and pepper. Set aside.

• Melt the butter in a saucepan. Add the endives and the sugar. Sauté over high heat until the endives are lightly caramelized and colored. Let cool in a bowl. Stack the endive leaves in four 10 cm (4 in.) ramequins to cover the inside wall. Fill with the lamb preparation and put aside.

• Preheat oven to 220°C (425°F) and place the puff pastry circles on a baking sheet lined with parchment paper. Put in the oven 8 min. Lower the temperature to 180°C (350°F) and cook 12 to 15 more min., until the pastry is well browned. Remove from the oven.

Cauliflower Purée: Bring the water and salt to a boil and cook the cauliflower. Drain and reduce to a smooth purée in the food processor. Add the butter and mix. Meanwhile, heat the cream and goat milk cheese in a saucepan, stirring often with a wooden spatula to obtain a uniform mixture. Pour onto the hot purée and stir 2 min. Check seasoning and keep warm.

Black Olive Emulsion: Melt the butter in a saucepan. Add the shallots and sweat until lightly colored. Deglaze with the red wine and reduce by half. Add the lamb stock, thyme and olives. Reduce by half, then remove the thyme sprigs. Mix in the blender at high speed 2 min. to obtain a smooth sauce. Pass through a sieve and add the butter and a little pepper. Put aside.

INGREDIENTS

LAMB TATIN
- 600 g (20 oz.) lamb shoulder, deboned
- 1 liter (4 cups) duck fat
- 2 white onions, thinly sliced
- 1 tablespoon butter
- 60 ml (¼ cup) olive oil
- Freshly ground salt and pepper
- 1 teaspoon butter
- Leaves of 2 endives, washed and dried
- 1 teaspoon sugar
- 4 12 by 0.5 cm (5 x ¼ in.) circles of puff pastry,

CAULIFLOWER PURÉE
- 1 liter (4 cups) water
- 1 teaspoon salt
- 200 g (1 cup) cauliflower flowerets
- 2 tablespoons butter
- 60 ml (¼ cup) cream
- 100 g (3⅓ oz.) goat milk cheese, Saint-Isidore or other
- Salt and white pepper

BLACK OLIVE EMULSION
- 1 tablespoon butter
- 2 gray shallots, chopped
- 75 ml (⅓ cup) red wine
- 175 ml (¾ cup) lamb stock or veal stock
- 2 sprigs of thyme
- 10 Kalamata olives, pitted
- 1 teaspoon unsalted butter
- Freshly ground pepper

GARNISH
- 12 string beans
- 1 teaspoon butter

Garnish: Blanch the string beans in salted water. Sauté in butter.

To Serve: Preheat oven to 230°C (450°F). Place the ramequins on the bottom rack 8 min. Place the puff pastry circles on each tatin and cook 2 more min. Meanwhile, pour the hot purée in the middle of individual plates. Turn the tatins over onto the purée and gently remove the ramequins. Top with a little black olive emulsion and garnish with string beans.

Rossini-style Sweetbreads

Serves 4

**Ask your butcher for milk-fed calf sweetbreads.
They cost a little more but their quality is second to none.**

Sweetbreads: Heat the butter in a saucepan and add the vegetables when it starts to froth. Sweat 5 min. Deglaze with the white wine, add the lemon, water, thyme, bay leaves and pepper. Simmer about 20 min. Place the sweetbreads in this broth and cook 15 min. over low heat. Turn off the heat, transfer into a bowl and let sit 30 min. Remove the sweetbreads from the broth and remove the skin covering. Cut into 4 slices and put aside in the refrigerator.

Sauce: Melt the butter in a saucepan. Add the shallots and sauté until lightly colored. Add the wine and reduce by half. Add the port and reduce by half. Add the veal stock and reduce to obtain a syrupy texture. Add the truffle cream. Stir, add salt and pepper as needed and keep warm.

Mashed Potatoes: Boil the potatoes 30 min. in salted water. Drain and pass through a potato ricer. Combine with the butter, cream, salt and pepper. Keep warm.

Pattypan Squash: Melt the butter in a saucepan. Add the squash, sun-dried tomatoes and oyster mushrooms. Sauté 5 min. Add the garlic, parsley, salt and pepper. Put aside.

Foie Gras: Add salt and pepper to the slices of foie gras on both sides. Heat a frying pan over very high heat and deposit the slices. Cook 1 min. on one side only until lightly browned. Remove from the pan and deposit the slices of sweetbread. Cook over medium heat until they are crunchy and well browned. Turn them over using a spatula and let them brown as before. Remove from the pan. Remove the leftover fat from the pan and turn the heat up to high. Cook the foie gras 1 min. on the uncooked side. Put aside.

PREPARATION

INGREDIENTS

SWEETBREADS
- 1 tablespoon butter
- 1 carrot, cut into 1 cm (1/2 in.) pieces
- 1 celery stalk, cut into 1 cm (1/2 in.) pieces
- 1 small onion, cut into 1 cm (1/2 in.) pieces
- 1/2 leek, cut into 1 cm (1/2 in.) pieces
- 125 ml (1/2 cup) white wine
- 1 lemon, quartered
- 1 liter (4 cups) water
- 1/2 teaspoon thyme
- 1 bay leaf
- 12 grains black pepper
- 400 g (14 oz.) sweetbreads

SAUCE
- 1 tablespoon butter
- 2 gray shallots, chopped
- 60 ml (1/4 cup) red wine
- 75 ml (1/3 cup) port
- 175 ml (3/4 cup) veal stock
- 1 tablespoon truffle cream
- Freshly ground salt and pepper

MASHED POTATOES
- 200 g (7 oz.) Yukon Gold potatoes, peeled
- 1 liter (4 cups) water
- Pinch of salt
- 60 ml (1/4 cup) butter
- 60 ml (1/4 cup) cream
- Salt and pepper

INGREDIENTS

PATTYPAN SQUASH

- 60 g (¼ cup) butter
- 8 pattypan squash, quartered
- 6 sun-dried tomatoes, cut into sticks
- 70 g (⅓ cup) oyster mushrooms, thinly sliced
- 1 garlic clove, crushed
- 1 teaspoon parsley
- Salt and pepper

FOIE GRAS

- 4 100 g (3½ oz.) slices of foie gras
- Freshly ground salt and pepper

PREPARATION

To Serve: On each individual plate, place a cookie cutter or round mold with a diameter of about 10 cm (4 in.). Put a slice of sweetbread in the cutter, then put the hot mashed potatoes on top. Garnish with a slice of foie gras. Carefully remove the cutter by sliding a knife blade on the inside wall. Collect the leftover butter from the foie gras and stir it into the well-heated sauce using a whisk. Top the foie gras with this sauce. Serve the pattypan squash on the side.

Provençal-style Marinated Rabbit Legs, Israeli Couscous With Lemon Oil and Candied Eggplant

Serves 4

This recipe is great for the barbecue. You can replace the rabbit with chicken. You'll find Israeli couscous at Indian and other specialty grocery stores.

Rabbit: Combine the vegetable juice, garlic, thyme, lemon, shallots and ketchup. Place in a bowl large enough to contain the rabbit legs. Let the legs marinate 3 hours in the refrigerator.

Candied Eggplant: Preheat oven to 200°C (400°F). Peel the eggplant and cut it into sticks the size of a french fry. Place in a bowl and add salt and pepper. Spread the eggplant on a baking sheet lined with parchment paper. Season with sugar and olive oil. Bake 12 min. in the oven and put aside.

Couscous: Place the couscous in a heatproof bowl. Add the lemon olive oil, parsley, garlic, salt and pepper. Meanwhile, bring the water and salt to a boil. Pour the boiling water onto the couscous. Cover the bowl with cellophane wrap and put aside.

Asparagus: In a skillet with the lid on, sauté the asparagus 5 min. over medium heat with butter, salt and pepper.

Cooking the Rabbit: Heat a frying pan over medium heat. Add a little olive oil and a knob of butter. Drain the rabbit legs (keep the marinade) and brown them 4 min. on each side. Finish cooking them in the oven 12 min. at 180°C (350°F).

To Serve: Reheat the eggplant 2 min. in the oven. Check if the couscous is still hot. Place two asparagus on each plate. Put a little couscous on top. Lean the rabbit leg on the couscous and serve the candied eggplant on the side. Boil the marinade 2 min. to reduce it by half. Pour a little marinade over the meat and serve.

INGREDIENTS

RABBIT
- 500 ml (2 cups) vegetable juice
- 2 garlic cloves, crushed
- 2 sprigs of fresh thyme
- 1 lemon, quartered
- 6 gray shallots, chopped
- 125 ml (½ cup) ketchup
- 4 rabbit legs
- Olive oil
- 1 knob of butter

CANDIED EGGPLANT
- 1 eggplant
- Freshly ground salt and pepper
- Sugar
- 75 ml (⅓ cup) olive oil

COUSCOUS
- 60 g (½ cup) Israeli couscous
- 60 ml (¼ cup) lemon-flavored olive oil
- 1 tablespoon fresh parsley, chopped
- 1 small garlic clove, chopped
- Freshly ground salt and pepper
- 250 ml (1 cup) water
- Pinch of salt

ASPARAGUS
- 8 asparagus, peeled
- 1 teaspoon butter
- Salt and pepper

Serves 4

INGREDIENTS

BEEF TENDERLOIN
- 6 very thin slices of Parma ham
- 2 tablespoons flat-leaved parsley, finely chopped
- 4 210 g (7 oz.) beef tenderloin medallions
- 1 tablespoon butter
- Salt and pepper

RED WINE JUICE
- 375 ml (1 ½ cup) red wine
- 2 gray shallots
- 125 ml (½ cup) veal stock
- 1 tablespoon sugar

POTATO FARIGOULE
- 80 g (⅓ cup) butter
- 60 ml (¼ cup) olive oil
- 480 g (1 lb.) potatoes, cut into 1 cm (½ in.) cubes
- 12 whole garlic cloves
- 1 tablespoon fresh thyme, chopped
- Freshly ground salt and pepper

TO SERVE
- Small season vegetables

PREPARATION

Add garlic paste inside the beef medallions for a stronger taste.

Beef Tenderloin: Garnish the slices of ham with parsley. Roll them into small sausages. Perforate the beef medallions in the direction of the sinews using a pointed utensil and insert the ham rolls. Keep in the refrigerator.

Red Wine Juice: In a small saucepan, heat the wine and shallots over high heat and reduce by half. Add the veal stock and sugar and reduce to a syrupy texture. Put aside for cooking the beef medallions.

Potato Farigoule: In a large non-stick pan, heat the butter and olive oil over medium-high heat until the butter is lightly colored. Add the potatoes. Brown over medium heat until they are half done. Add the garlic cloves and cook a few minutes, stirring well to prevent them from burning. When the potatoes are cooked, add the thyme, salt and pepper. Put aside.

Cooking the Beef: Put the remaining butter in a heavy saucepan. Add salt and pepper to the beef medallions and brown over medium heat to give them a nice color. Put in the oven a few minutes depending on how done you like them to be. Baste them with the red wine juice using a brush or spoon.

To Serve: Sauté a few small vegetables in butter and place them on individual plates. Cut the beef medallions in two and place them beside the vegetables. Garnish with the heated potatoes. Serve with the red wine juice.

Boileau Venison Osso Bucco Braised in a Parsnip and Date Compote, Risotto Croquettes and Coriander Gremolata

Serves 4

You can replace the white wine with red wine to cook the risotto. Add a quartered beet to cook up a delightfully purplish risotto.

Osso Bucco: Place a flameproof saucepan over high heat. Add the butter until lightly hazelnut colored. Meanwhile, add salt and pepper on both sides of the meat. When the butter starts to brown, sear the meat quickly on both sides. Deglaze with the wine and veal stock. Add the garlic and thyme. Cook 5 hours in the oven at 150°C (300°F).

Risotto Croquettes: Meanwhile, combine the risotto with the chives and tomatoes. Separate into four equal parts and shape the croquettes. Brown lightly in butter.

Parsnip and Date Compote: Bring the water and salt to a boil in a large saucepan. Cook the parsnips about 10 min. and drain. In a saucepan, combine the dates, parsnips, cream, Parmesan cheese and butter. Add salt and pepper and cook 10 min. to turn the mixture into a compote. Stir often using a wooden spatula to prevent the Parmesan cheese from sticking to the pan.

Gremolata: Combine all the ingredients in a small pot and put aside.

To Serve: Reheat the risotto croquettes about 10 min. in the oven at 180°C (350°F). Pour the hot compote into bowls or deep plates and place the osso bucco on top. Top with the cooking juices of the meat using a service spoon. Garnish each serving with a risotto croquette. Sprinkle with gremolata and serve.

INGREDIENTS

OSSO BUCCO
- 1 tablespoon butter
- Salt and pepper
- 4 osso buccos of Boileau venison or other
- 250 ml (1 cup) red wine
- 1 liter (4 cups) veal stock
- 1 garlic clove
- Sprig of thyme

RISOTTO CROQUETTES
- 160 g (1 cup) basic risotto (p. 89)
- 2 tablespoons chives
- 4 tablespoons diced tomatoes
- 60 g (¼ cup) butter

PARSNIP AND DATE COMPOTE
- 500 ml (2 cups) water
- 1 teaspoon salt
- 3 parsnips, cut into 1 cm (½ in.) pieces
- 60 g (⅓ cup) dates, thinly sliced
- 75 ml (⅓ cup) cream
- 2 tablespoons Parmesan cheese
- 1 tablespoon butter
- Salt and pepper

GREMOLATA
- 2 tablespoons fresh coriander, chopped
- Zest of one lemon
- 1 garlic clove, chopped

Roasted Milk-fed Veal Liver With a Spice Coating, Yellow Carrot Purée With Beurre Noisette, Turnips Cooked in Duck Fat With Cinnamon

Serves 4

INGREDIENTS

YELLOW CARROT PURÉE
- 400 g (2 cups) yellow carrots, cut into pieces
- 1 liter (4 cups) water
- 80 g (⅓ cup) butter
- Salt and white pepper
- 1 tablespoon heavy cream (35 %)

TURNIPS
- 12 small turnips, peeled
- 250 ml (1 cup) duck fat
- 3 cinnamon sticks
- Salt and white pepper

SAUCE
- 60 ml (¼ cup) veal stock
- 1 tablespoon red wine vinegar
- Salt and pepper

VEAL LIVER
- 1 teaspoon curry
- ½ teaspoon ginger
- 1 teaspoon cumin
- 1 teaspoon aniseed
- 1 teaspoon allspice
- 2 tablespoons butter
- 2 tablespoons oil
- Freshly ground salt and pepper
- 4 200 g (7 oz.) pieces of milk-fed veal liver
- 1 tablespoon warm honey

PREPARATION

Buy whole spices if you can and grind them with a coffee grinder. The flavor and smell of hand-ground spices is unbeatable. You can also serve this dish with miniature potatoes sautéed in butter with finely chopped shallots.

Yellow Carrot Purée: Cook the carrots 20 min. in salted boiling water and reduce to a purée in the food processor. In a frying pan, heat the butter over medium heat until lightly colored. Add the carrots, salt, pepper and cream. Stir 1 min. Add salt and pepper as needed.

Turnips: Put the turnips in a pot. Add the duck fat, cinnamon, salt and pepper. Cover and cook 30 min. in the oven at 200°C (400°F). Take the pot out of the oven and let cool with the turnips inside.

Sauce: Combine the veal stock, wine vinegar, salt and pepper. Bring to a boil. Add salt and pepper as needed and put aside.

Veal Liver: Combine the curry, ginger, cumin, aniseed and allspice. (If you use whole spices, grind them first in the coffee grinder.) Put a frying pan over medium heat. Add the butter and oil and melt them gently. When the butter starts to froth, add salt and pepper to the veal liver and brown about 1 min. on each side. Place in the oven 8 min. at 200°C (400°F) turning it every 2 min. to cook it evenly. Take out of the oven, brush it with warm honey and roll it in the spices.

To Serve: Put some carrot purée on individual plates. Place a piece of warm veal liver on top. Garnish with turnips all around and top with the sauce.

Milk-fed Veal Chops Cooked in Beurre Noisette, Veal Juice With Beurre Noisette and Hazelnut Cream

Serves 4

Make sure the beurre noisette and hazelnut preparations are not rancid before using them.

Hazelnut Cream: Melt the butter in a saucepan. Add the green onions and stir using a wooden spoon until caramelized. Add the hazelnuts and sauté 1 min. Deglaze with the white wine and reduce by half. Add the chicken stock and reduce by half. Add the cream and mix in the blender 2 min. to obtain a smooth, creamy texture. Add salt and pepper and put aside.

Veal Juice with Beurre Noisette: Pour the wine in a saucepan and reduce by half over high heat. Add the veal stock and reduce by half. In another saucepan, heat the butter over high heat until it is hazelnut colored. Transfer into the first saucepan, add salt and pepper as needed and put aside.

Veal Chops: In a frying pan (cast iron if possible), melt the butter until it starts to froth. Add the garlic cloves and thyme. Season the veal chops and brown them over medium heat on both sides until colored. Put them in the oven 10 min. at 230°C (450°F) and put aside.

Potatoes: Cook the potatoes 15 to 20 min. in salted water. Drain using a strainer. Heat a frying pan over high heat. Add the bacon and butter and sauté lightly. Add the potatoes, hazelnuts and aragula. Add salt and pepper. Sauté and put aside.

Garnish: Put the potatoes on individual plates. Garnish with a veal chop. Top with a little veal juice and hazelnut cream. Add salt and pepper and serve with snow peas.

INGREDIENTS

HAZELNUT CREAM
- 1 tablespoon butter
- 2 green onions, chopped
- 40 g (⅓ cup) hazelnuts, shelled
- 75 ml (⅓ cup) white wine
- 75 ml (⅓ cup) white chicken stock
- 75 ml (⅓ cup) heavy cream (35 %)
- 2 tablespoons salt
- White pepper

VEAL JUICE WITH BEURRE NOISETTE
- 125 ml (½ cup) red wine
- 175 ml (¾ cup) veal stock
- 120 g (½ cup) unsalted butter

VEAL CHOPS
- Butter
- 3 garlic cloves
- 4 sprigs of thyme
- 4 milk-fed veal chops

POTATOES
- 16 new small potatoes, quartered
- 1 liter (4 cups) water
- 1/2 teaspoon salt
- 45 g (¼ cup) bacon, thinly sliced
- 2 tablespoons butter
- 36 hazelnuts, shelled
- 100 g (2 cups) aragula
- Fleur de sel
- Freshly ground pepper

GARNISH
- 8 snow peas
- Salt and pepper

Québec Lamb Shank Braised in Tandoori, Sweet Potato Fries and Stir-Fried Vegetables With Olive Oil

Serves 4

INGREDIENTS

LAMB SHANKS
- 4 lamb shanks from Québec
- 2 tablespoons tandoori
- 200 ml (¾ cup + 1 tablespoon) red wine
- 2 garlic cloves
- 4 sprigs of thyme
- 500 ml (2 cups) lamb stock or veal stock

SWEET POTATO FRIES
- 3 big sweet potatoes, peeled and cut into fries
- Frying oil
- Pinch of salt
- Pinch of allspice

VINAIGRETTE
- 75 ml (⅓ cup) olive oil
- 2 tablespoons lemon juice
- 2 tablespoons white wine
- 1 teaspoon fresh coriander, finely chopped
- 1 teaspoon curry
- Salt and pepper

VEGETABLE STIR-FRY
- 12 cippolini onions, peeled
- 6 miniature turnips, peeled
- 6 big button mushrooms
- 12 sweet peas
- 12 miniature carrots, peeled
- 200 g (1 cup) spinach
- 3 green onions
- 1 knob of butter
- 12 Kalamata olives, pitted

PREPARATION

Cook the shanks the day before and let them cool in the cooking juices so they soak up the stock. That way, they will be juicier when you serve them.

Lamb Shanks: Place the shanks in a Pyrex bowl. In another bowl, put the tandoori, wine, garlic and thyme. Stir well and pour over the meat. Keep 6 hours in the refrigerator, turning the shanks over in the marinade once an hour so they are well impregnated. Place the shanks in a large flameproof saucepan. Pour the marinade over the meat, add the lamb stock and cook 6 hours in the oven at 160°C (325°F). When they are done, take the dish out of the oven and check that the meat breaks apart easily using a fork. If they are not quite done, put them back in the oven 30 to 60 min. depending on the size of the shanks. Leave them in the broth when you take them out of the oven.

Sweet Potato Fries: Put the fries in the deep fryer to pre-cook them. When you are ready to serve, put them back in the deep fryer until they are golden. Place in a dish lined with paper towels to remove excess oil. Add salt and allspice.

Vinaigrette: Combine the oil, lemon juice and wine. Add the coriander, curry, salt and pepper. Whisk thoroughly and add salt and pepper as needed. Put aside.

Stir-Fried Vegetables: Bring 1 liter (4 cups) water and a pinch of salt to a boil. Blanch all the vegetables except the olives until they are al dente. Drain thoroughly. Put the butter in a saucepan. When it starts to froth, sauté the vegetables and olives. Deglaze with the vinaigrette and keep warm.

To Serve: Place the well-heated shanks on individual plates. Garnish with fries and serve the vegetables on the side. Top with a little sauce and serve.

Veal Tenderloin Poached in Olive Oil, Potato and Artichoke Cake with Roasted Garlic, Cream of Caramelized Onion With Port and Butter

Serves 4

Avoid overheating the olives. They will lose their good taste and characteristics.

Artichoke Cakes: Remove the artichoke leaves and heart. Peel completely and keep only the base. Using a spoon, scrape and remove the beards. Cut the artichoke into strips and place in a bowl. Heat the olive oil in a non-stick pan. Add the artichoke strips and sauté 2 min. Add the garlic and sauté 30 sec. Deglaze with the lemon juice. Add salt and pepper and heat 1 more min. Put aside in a bowl.

• Peel the potato and grate it using a cheese grater. Combine with the artichokes and add salt and pepper to taste. Line four ramequins with cellophane wrap. Divide the artichokes up into four portions and fill the ramequins. Press firmly to remove excess juice and close the cellophane wrap. Keep at least 1 hour in the refrigerator.

Cream of Onion: In a saucepan, melt the butter and olive oil. When the butter starts to froth, sauté the onions 10 min. over medium heat until they are caramelized. Add salt and pepper and mix 5 min. in the food processor to obtain a smooth purée. Put aside.

Port Sauce: Melt the butter in a saucepan. Sauté the shallots until lightly colored. Deglaze with the port. Add the cream and reduce by half, adding the butter at the last second. Whisk briskly and put aside.

Garnish: Cook the pearl onions in the port and butter with a little salt and pepper. (To see if they are done, insert the tip of a knife in the flesh just like another other vegetable.) Peel the miniature artichokes in the same way as for the artichoke cakes. Sauté with olive oil, wine and lemon juice. Add salt and pepper. Cook 7 to 8 min. and put aside.

Green Olive Tapenade: Combine all the ingredients in the blender to obtain a uniform texture. Put aside in a bowl.

To Serve: Remove the artichoke cakes from the mold and peel off the cellophane wrap. Heat a non-stick pan and add a little butter and olive oil. When the butter is a little frothy, gently place the cakes in the pan and cook over medium heat until lightly colored. Cook 20 min. in the oven at 180°C (350°F) and put aside.

INGREDIENTS

ARTICHOKE CAKES
- 3 artichokes
- 60 ml (¼ cup) olive oil
- 1 garlic clove, chopped
- 1 tablespoon lemon juice
- Salt and pepper
- 1 small potato

CREAM OF ONION
- 2 tablespoons butter
- 60 ml (¼ cup) olive oil
- 3 onions, thinly sliced
- Freshly ground salt and pepper

PORT SAUCE
- 1 teaspoon butter
- 2 gray shallots, finely chopped
- 125 ml (½ cup) port
- 60 ml (¼ cup) cream
- 60 g (¼ cup) unsalted butter, cut into small cubes

GARNISH
- 12 pearl onions, peeled
- 125 ml (½ cup) port
- 1 teaspoon butter
- Freshly ground salt and pepper
- 1 tablespoon olive oil
- 60 ml (¼ cup) white wine
- Juice of one lemon
- 2 sprigs of tarragon

GREEN OLIVE TAPENADE

- 30 g (¼ cup) green olives
- 1 small garlic clove
- 1 teaspoon lemon juice
- 1 teaspoon hot mustard
- 2 tablespoons olive oil

VEAL TENDERLOINS

- 1 liter (4 cups) olive oil
- 4 180 g (6 oz.) veal tenderloins
- Freshly ground salt and pepper

Veal Tenderloins: Meanwhile, heat the olive oil over medium heat in a deep saucepan. Add salt and pepper to the tenderloins and drop them in the hot oil. Lower the heat to medium-low (quivering) and poach gently 8 to 10 min. or more if you prefer not to serve them pink. When the tenderloins are ready, remove them from the oil. The artichoke cakes should be ready to take out of the oven at the same time. Reheat the cream of onion and the port sauce and gently heat the garnish.

To Serve: Fry the tarragon sprigs a few seconds in hot oil. Pour the cream of onion into small bowls. Put three small onions cooked in port on top. Place a tenderloin in the middle of individual plates and garnish with the olive tapenade shaped into a quenelle. Put an artichoke cake on the side and garnish with fried miniature artichokes. Finish with a drizzle of port sauce, garnish with the fried tarragon and serve.

Québec Piglet Loin With Mustard, Maple Sugar and Parmesan Cheese Coating, Candied Tomato Tart

Serves 4

INGREDIENTS

MUSTARD COATING
- 3 teaspoons Dijon mustard
- 2 tablespoons maple sugar
- 2 tablespoons Parmesan cheese, freshly grated

TART
- 8 tomatoes
- 1 liter (4 cups) water
- Freshly ground salt and pepper
- Pinch of salt
- 2 tablespoons olive oil
- Puff pastry
- 4 piglet loins
- 60 ml (¼ cup) olive oil
- 1 leek, thinly sliced

SAUCE
- 175 ml (¾ cup) veal stock
- 1 tablespoon tomato paste
- 1 teaspoon honey

PREPARATION

If you don't have puff pastry handy, use a homemade short crust pastry made from butter.

Mustard Coating: Combine all the ingredients in a bowl and put aside.

Tart: Remove the pedicel from the tomatoes and make a cross-shaped incision at the other end using a knife. Bring the water and salt to a boil in a saucepan. Plunge the tomatoes 30 sec. in the boiling water and plunge them immediately in a bowl of ice water. Remove the peels. Quarter the tomatoes. Remove the seeds and place the tomatoes on a baking sheet. Cover with salt, pepper, sugar and olive oil. Put them in the oven 1 hour at 120°C (250°F). Put aside.

• Cut the puff pastry using a cutter or knife to make four 12 cm (5 in.) circles with a thickness of 0.5 cm (¼ in.). Bake them 20 min. in the oven at 190°C (375°F). Add salt and pepper to the piglet loins. Heat a frying pan over medium-high heat. Add the olive oil. When it starts to fume, sear the loins 1 min. on each side. Put them 5 min. in the oven preheated to 200°C (400°F). Remove from the oven and put aside. In the same pan, add the leeks and cook 5 min. over medium heat. Add salt and pepper and put aside.

Sauce: Heat the veal stock, the tomato paste and the honey. Add salt and pepper as needed and put aside.

To Serve: Place the puff pastry on a baking sheet and cover with the leeks and candied tomatoes. Brush the loins with the mustard coating preparation to form a 1 cm (½ in.) thick coating. Place the loins on a baking sheet and put them 3 min. in the oven preheated to Broil (top rack). On the bottom rack, place the baking sheet with the puff pastries. Spread a little sauce on a plate and put a hot pastry in the middle. Cut each loin into three equal pieces and place them on top.

Sweet and Sour Rib of Beef, Fennel, Chili and Mango Salad

Serves 4

**Before serving the ribs, put them on the barbecue
2 minutes on each side to give them a light smoky taste.**

Ribs: Combine the honey, ketchup, rice vinegar, miso and veal stock in a bowl for the refrigerator. Add the ribs and macerate about 2 hours.

Fennel, Chili and Mango Salad: Combine all the ingredients in a large bowl and keep in the refrigerator.

Cooking the Ribs: Place the ribs on a baking dish. Top with the marinade and cook 3½ hours at 150°C (300°F). (The meat should break apart easily with a fork.) Several times during cooking, brush the ribs with a little sauce using a spoon so they are well glazed.

To Serve: Put a little fennel salad on individual plates, add two ribs and serve.

INGREDIENTS

RIBS
- 60 ml (⅓ cup) honey
- 2 tablespoons ketchup
- 60 ml (⅓ cup) rice vinegar
- 2 tablespoons miso
- 500 ml (2 cups) veal stock
- 8 ribs

FENNEL, CHILI AND MANGO SALAD
- 2 fennel bulbs, thinly sliced
- 1 fresh mango, cut into sticks
- 60 ml (¼ cup) sweet and sour chili sauce
- 1 tablespoon rice vinegar
- 1 teaspoon sesame oil
- 60 ml (¼ cup) canola oil
- Freshly ground salt and pepper

Plum Shooter With Blue Cheese and Whipped Almond Milk Cream

Serves 4

Tell your guests to stir all the ingredients thoroughly before sipping!

Plum Purée: Mix the plums 2 min. in the blender to obtain a very smooth purée. Pass through a sieve and put aside in the refrigerator.

Blue Cheese Cream: Mix the blue cheese and quark cheese in the food processor to obtain a very smooth texture. Place in a pastry bag and put aside.

Whipped Almond Milk: Roast the powdered almonds 2 min. in the oven at 200°C (400°F). Remove from the oven. Meanwhile, bring the milk to a boil in a saucepan. Add the powdered almonds to the milk and heat 1 min. Turn off the heat and stir well. Let cool. Whip the cream until three quarters done and combine with the milk. Whip again a few times until it is firm.

To Serve: Using a spoon, pour the plum purée into shooter glasses. Put the blue cheese cream on top and garnish with the whipped almond milk.

PLUM PURÉE
- 3 ripe plums (Reida if possible), cut into two, pitted and cut into two once again

BLUE CHEESE CREAM
- 30 g (¼ cup) Benedictine Blue Cheese from Saint-Benoît-du-Lac or other blue cheese, cut into small pieces
- 2 tablespoons quark cheese

WHIPPED ALMOND MILK
- 2 tablespoons powdered almonds
- 60 ml (¼ cup) milk
- 75 ml (⅓ cup) heavy cream (35 %)

Tournevent Goat Cheese Bricks, Candied Pears and Clove-flavored Honey Caramel

Serves 4

INGREDIENTS

GOAT CHEESE BRICKS
- 4 spring roll pastries
- 300 g (10 oz.) Tournevent goat milk cheese or other
- 1 tablespoon water
- Flour
- Frying oil

CANDIED PEARS
- 375 ml (1½ cup) water
- 60 g (¼ cup) sugar
- 125 ml (½ cup) white wine
- 4 pears, dried, peeled and emptied

CLOVE-FLAVORED HONEY CARAMEL
- 100 g (¼ cup) honey
- ½ teaspoon ground cloves

TO SERVE
- A few oak leaves
- 12 whole cloves

PREPARATION

This dish can be served as an entrée or after the main course with a few shoots of corn salad.

Goat Cheese Bricks: Separate the spring roll pastries and roll them out with the point towards you. Put some goat cheese in the middle of each one. Combine the water and flour to make a 'glue' and apply it to the upper tip of the pastry. Bring the lower tip up onto the cheese in the middle. Then bring the left and right tips to the center of the roll and roll up to the upper tip. Make sure the glue on the tip sticks to the rest of the roll. Keep in the refrigerator.

Candied Pears: In a saucepan, add the water, sugar and wine over medium-high heat. Add the pears and cook about 15 min. (The tip of a knife inserted into the flesh should come easily.) Drain and let cool in the refrigerator.

Honey Caramel: In a small saucepan, heat the honey over high heat. Add the cloves and stir well. When the cloves start to fume and the honey starts to caramelize, remove from heat and pour into a small bowl.

To Serve: Drop the goat cheese bricks 1½ min. in frying oil until the batter is lightly colored or put in the oven 5 min. at 200°C (400°F). Cut the bricks in two and put them on individual plates. Garnish with candied pears, add a few oak leaves and cloves to decorate and finish with a spoonful of honey caramel.

Pont Couvert Cheese Roll With Chestnuts, Grated Honey Carrots

Serves 4

Use fresh chestnuts if you can for this recipe to avoid melting them during cooking.

Short Crust Pastry: Combine the flour with the baking powder. Add the butter and rub the mixture between your hands to obtain a sandy flour. Combine the water and the salt and slowly add the flour. Put the pastry 30 min. in the refrigerator.

Grated Honey Carrots: Combine the carrots with the oil, honey, pistachios, salt, pepper and chives. Add salt and pepper as needed. Add the lemon juice. Marinate 30 min. in the refrigerator.

Rolls: Spread the short crust pastry to a thickness of 0.5 cm (½ in.) and make into 2 15 x 20 cm (6 x 8 in.) rectangles. Spread a little chestnut purée in the middle and cover with the cheese. Brush the edges of the pastry with egg yolk. Roll the pastry into a sausage, taking care to seal the ends and edges so the cheese does not run during cooking. Preheat the oven to 190°C (375°F). Cook the rolls 15 min. and then cut them in two. Serve a half roll per plate, accompanied with a small mound of carrots. Decorate with the carrot tops.

INGREDIENTS

SHORT CRUST PASTRY
- 180 g (1 cup) flour
- ½ teaspoon baking powder
- 120 g (½ cup) softened butter
- 4 tablespoons water
- Pinch of salt

GRATED HONEY CARROTS
- 2 carrots, peeled and finely grated (keep a few tops)
- 60 ml (¼ cup) olive oil
- 1 tablespoon honey
- 2 tablespoons pistachios, chopped
- Freshly ground salt and pepper
- 1 teaspoon chives, chopped
- Juice of one lemon

ROLLS
- 125 ml (½ cup) chestnut purée
- 300 g (10 oz.) 'Pont Couvert' cheese, sliced 2 cm (1 in.) thick
- 2 egg yolks, beaten

RESTAURANT
CHEZ L'ÉPICIER
Nº311
ST-PAUL EST
MTL
ET BAR À VIN

Clementine and Ground Cherry Soup With Monbazillac, Frozen Cinnamon Fondant

Serves 4

Let the clementines macerate at least 6 hours to let them soak up the syrup flavor.

Soup: Heat the clementine juice with the sugar. Add the Monbazillac. Combine with the clementines and ground cherries and refrigerate 1 hour.

Fondant: Whip the cream. Add the icing sugar and cinnamon and pour into individual molds. Freeze about 4 hours. Remove from the molds and place in dishes or individual bowls. Pour the soup on top. Decorate each portion with fresh mint, a cinnamon stick and a ground cherry.

INGREDIENTS

SOUP
- 750 ml (3 cups) clementine juice
- 60 g (¼ cup) sugar
- 150 ml (⅔ cup) Monbazillac
- 3 clementines, in slices
- 20 ground cherries, cut in two

FONDANT
- 300 ml (1¼ cup) whipping cream
- 80 g (½ cup) icing sugar
- ½ teaspoon cinnamon

GARNISH
- Fresh mint leaves
- 4 cinnamon sticks
- 4 ground cherries

Apple Pecan Crumble With Rosemary, Vanilla Mousseline

Serves 4

INGREDIENTS

VANILLA MOUSSELINE
- 1 tablespoon corn starch
- 60 g (1/4 cup) sugar
- 3 eggs
- 250 ml (1 cup) milk
- 1 vanilla pod, cut in two
- 125 ml (1/2 cup) heavy semi-whipped cream (35 %)

CRUMBLE PREPARATION
- 90 g (1/4 cup) flour
- 80 g (1/3 cup) sugar
- 80 g (1/3 cup) butter, melted
- 40 g (1/3 cup) pecans, ground
- 1 teaspoon fresh rosemary, chopped

CARAMELIZED APPLES
- 60 g (1/4 cup) butter
- 60 g (1/4 cup) maple sugar
- 6 Golden Delicious apples, cored and quartered

PREPARATION

If you prepare the crumble ahead of time, serve it hot. It's much tastier that way!

Vanilla Mousseline: In a bowl, combine the corn starch, sugar and eggs using a whisk. Put the milk in a saucepan over medium-high heat. Add the vanilla and heat just to the boiling point. Remove from the heat, add to the first preparation and stir. Transfer the mixture into a saucepan, put back on the heat 4 to 5 min. and keep boiling while stirring with a wooden spoon to keep the cream from sticking. Remove the vanilla. Pour the mixture into a bowl and let cool about 20 min. Add the semi-whipped cream and stir well using a whisk to obtain a smooth and uniform cream. Keep in the refrigerator.

Crumble Preparation: Combine the flour, sugar and butter. Add the pecans and rosemary and stir well.

Caramelized Apples: Put a frying pan over high heat with the butter and maple sugar. When they are lightly colored, sauté the apples 5 min. to color them. Pour into a cooking dish with a depth of at least 5 cm (2 in.) and spread the crumble preparation over top. Put in the oven about 15 min. at 200°C (400°F) until lightly colored.

To Serve: Pour the mousseline into small serving pots or spread it on individual plates. Cut the crumble up into squares and place on the plates using a spatula.

Chocolate Club Sandwich,
Pineapple Fries and Creamy Melon Salad

Serves 4

Use very ripe and flavorful pineapples. Make sure you fry them in a deep fryer or deep saucepan.

Cake: Preheat the oven to 180°C (350°F). In the electric mixer bowl, put the eggs and beat 30 sec. Add the butter and beat 2 more min. Add the sugar and flour to obtain a creamy texture. Spread onto a large baking sheet at a thickness of 0.5 cm (½ in.) and bake in the oven 7 to 8 min. Put aside.

Crème Anglaise: In a saucepan, heat the milk over medium-high heat just to the boiling point. Meanwhile, briskly whisk the egg yolks and sugar in a large bowl to obtain a creamy mousse. Add the boiling milk and stir well. Reheat 30 sec. and remove from heat.

Dark Chocolate Mousse: Combine half the warm crème anglaise with the dark chocolate. Make sure it is completely melted. Let sit at room temperature and put aside. Whip the cream until it is three quarters done and add it to the preparation.

Mounting: Cut the cake into three rectangles of equal size. Make a mold out of aluminum foil with a width of 4 cm (1½ in.) that will completely enclose the first piece of cake. Place the first piece of cake on the bottom of the mold and pour the dark chocolate mousse on top. Place the second piece of cake on top. Keep 30 min. in the refrigerator.

White Chocolate Mousse: Meanwhile, soak the gelatine in cold water. Combine the rest of the warm crème anglaise with the white chocolate. Wring out the water from the leaf of gelatine and add it to the crème anglaise. Let sit at room temperature. When the preparation is lukewarm, whip the cream until it is three quarters done and add it to the preparation. Pour onto the cake from the refrigerator and place the third piece of cake on top. Keep 3 hours in the refrigerator.

Pineapple Fries: Combine the fries with the cornmeal. Put aside in the refrigerator.

Creamy Melon Salad: Combine the melon, yogurt, honey and mint. Put into small salad bowls and keep in the refrigerator.

CAKE
- 75 ml (⅓ cup) eggs
- 80 g (⅓ cup) softened butter
- 80 g (⅓ cup) sugar
- 60 g (⅓ cup) flour

CRÈME ANGLAISE
- 250 ml (1 cup) milk
- 3 egg yolks
- 1 tablespoon sugar

DARK CHOCOLATE MOUSSE
- 120 g (⅓ cup) dark chocolate
- 100 ml (⅓ cup + 2 tablespoons) heavy cream (35 %)

WHITE CHOCOLATE MOUSSE
- 1 gelatine leaf
- 120 g (⅓ cup) white chocolate, melted
- 100 ml (⅓ cup + 2 tablespoons) heavy cream (35 %)

PINEAPPLE FRIES
- 16 pieces of pineapple, cut into fries
- 125 ml (½ cup) cornmeal
- Frying oil
- Pinch of sugar

CREAMY MELON SALAD

- 1 piece of honeydew melon, cut into sticks
- 80 g (⅓ cup) yogurt
- 1 tablespoon honey
- 1 teaspoon fresh mint, chopped

FINAL STEPS

- Basil leaves
- Strawberries, thinly sliced

Mounting the Cake: Take the cake out of the refrigerator and remove the aluminum foil. Cut the cake up into 8 cm (3 in.) squares. Turn the cake onto its side and, using a knife, separate the white and dark chocolate mousses. Spread basil leaves and thin strawberry slices on the white chocolate mousse. Rebuild the club sandwich by replacing the dark chocolate cake on top. Prick toothpicks into the four corners as you would for a club sandwich. Drop the pineapple fries into the frying oil about 1 min. until lightly colored. Drain on a paper towel and add a little sugar.

To Serve: Cut the sandwich diagonally into four pieces. Serve on a plate with two pieces on each side, a few fries and a small bowl with the melon salad.

Chocolate Ginger Tart, Pear Juice Crème Anglaise

Serves 4

Most recipe books use ground ginger in dessert recipes. Personally, I prefer using fresh ginger. All you have to do is reduce the required quantity by half. What a difference!

Pie Crust: Combine the icing sugar, flour, salt and orange zest. Add the butter and stir well as for a pie dough. Add the egg and keep 1 hour in the refrigerator. Spread the dough into tart molds or one large pie pan. Bake in the oven at 180°C (350°F) until the edges start to brown. Let sit at room temperature.

Chocolate Ginger Ganache: In a saucepan, heat the cream just to the boiling point. Turn off the heat. Add the chocolate and stir well to melt it. Pour into a bowl. Add the ginger, egg yolk and butter. Stir well and pour over the crust. Refrigerate until ready to serve.

Pear Juice Crème Anglaise: Peel the pear into small sticks and put aside. Place the peels and leftovers in a saucepan with the water and sugar. Heat just to the boiling point. Filter the syrup into a bowl and add the pear sticks. Let soak about 20 min. Remove the pear sticks. Combine the syrup with the cream and egg yolks. Put the preparation back into a saucepan over medium heat and stir gently using a wooden spoon until it thickens lightly. Remove immediately from the heat. When the cream coats the spoon, pour into a bowl and place in the refrigerator.

To Serve: Serve the tart with the pear sticks and a little crème anglaise.

INGREDIENTS

PIE CRUST
- 75 g (½ cup) icing sugar
- 180 g (1 cup) flour
- Pinch of salt
- Zest of one orange
- 120 g (½ cup) softened butter
- 1 egg

CHOCOLATE GINGER GANACHE
- 125 ml (½ cup) heavy cream (35 %)
- 180 ml (⅔ cup) dark chocolate, in small pieces (pure Caraibe from Valrhona or other)
- 1 teaspoon fresh ginger, grated
- 1 egg yolk
- 1 teaspoon unsalted butter

PEAR JUICE CREME ANGLAISE
- 1 well-ripened pear
- 75 ml (⅓ cup) water
- 80 g (⅓ cup) sugar
- 125 ml (½ cup) heavy cream (35 %)
- 4 egg yolks

Frozen Chocolate Blin Sandwiches With Crushed Strawberries and Cream
Just Like My Mother Taught Me

Serves 3

To keep the strawberries fresh, prepare the crushed strawberries only at the last minute.

Blins: Melt the dark chocolate, the white chocolate and the butter in a double boiler. Whip the egg whites with the sugar using an electric mixer to obtain a tight gleaming meringue. Fold the meringue into the melted chocolate using a rubber spatula. Bake on a deep baking sheet lined with parchment paper. Cut into six small circles.

Chocolate Mousse: Melt the chocolate in a double boiler. When it is completely melted and hot, transfer it into a large bowl and add half the semi-whipped cream. Stir well and add the rest of the cream. Put aside. In another bowl, combine the egg yolks with the sugar to obtain a creamy texture. Combine with the chocolate preparation and whipped cream. Place three blins on a freezer-proof baking sheet. Garnish with a little chocolate mousse and add another blin on top. Keep 1 hour in the freezer.

Crushed Strawberries: Put the strawberries in a bowl with the sugar and port. Crush using a fork. When the texture is that of a compote, add the fresh cream and stir. Put aside.

Chocolate Syrup: In a saucepan, bring the water and sugar to a boil over high heat. Turn off the heat and add the chocolate, cocoa and butter. Stir well.

To Serve: Take the blins out of the freezer and place them in the middle of the plates. Garnish with a little crushed strawberries and decorate with the chocolate syrup.

INGREDIENTS

BLINS
- 220 g (7 ⅓ oz.) dark chocolate
- 200 g (7 oz.) white chocolate
- 120 g (½ cup) butter
- 300 g (10 oz.) egg whites
- 120 g (½ cup) sugar

CHOCOLATE MOUSSE
- 60 g (⅓ cup) bittersweet chocolate (70 % cocoa)
- 125 ml (½ cup) semi-whipped cream
- 2 egg yolks
- 60 g (¼ cup) sugar

CRUSHED STRAWBERRIES
- 150 g (¾ cup) strawberries, washed and hulled
- 1 teaspoon sugar
- 1 tablespoon sweet white port
- 2 tablespoons fresh cream

CHOCOLATE SYRUP
- 2 tablespoons water
- 2 tablespoons sugar
- 45 g (¼ cup) chocolate
- 1 tablespoon cocoa powder
- 1 teaspoon unsalted butter

INGREDIENTS

CHOCOLATE SAUCE
- 75 ml (⅓ cup) cream
- 60 g (⅓ cup) chocolate

CARAMEL SAUCE
- 125 ml (½ cup) honey
- 2 tablespoons pineapple juice

TO SERVE
- 30 hazelnuts
- 1 well-ripened pineapple, peeled and quartered
- Premium quality vanilla ice cream
- 75 ml (⅓ cup) sweet whipped cream
- 12 fresh cherries

PREPARATION

As nuts tend to go rancid quickly, buy small quantities at a time.

Hazelnuts: Preheat the oven to 190°C (375°F) and roast the hazelnuts 10 min. Let sit at room temperature, then rub them in a cloth to rid them of their peels. Put aside.

Chocolate Sauce: In a saucepan, bring the cream to a boil. Add the chocolate. Remove from heat and stir lightly until the chocolate is melted. Put aside.

Caramel Sauce: In a saucepan, bring the honey to a boil until lightly caramelized. When the sauce darkens a little, deglaze with the pineapple juice. Remove from heat, stir well and put aside.

To Serve: Put the pineapple on a plate. Cover with scoops of ice cream. Garnish with a little whipped cream, cherries and roasted hazelnuts. Top with chocolate sauce and caramel sauce.

Spice Cakes, Semi-Sour Semi-Whipped Cream, Fudge Sauce, Hot Maple Taffy Milk

Serves 4

CAKES
- 135 g (¾ cup) pastry flour, sifted
- ¼ teaspoon baking powder
- ¼ teaspoon baking soda
- 1 teaspoon salt
- 1 teaspoon cinnamon
- ¼ teaspoon allspice
- ¼ teaspoon nutmeg
- ⅛ teaspoon ground cloves
- 30 g (⅛ cup) vegetable fat
- 120 g (½ cup) sugar
- 1 egg
- 1 teaspoon vanilla
- 100 ml (⅓ cup + 2 tablespoons) milk

FUDGE SAUCE
- 60 ml (½ cup) heavy cream (35 %)
- 50 g (¼ cup) brown sugar
- 60 g (¼ cup) white sugar

SEMI-SOUR SEMI-WHIPPED CREAM
- 125 ml (½ cup) sour cream
- 1 teaspoon ground allspice
- 2 tablespoons icing sugar
- 125 ml (½ cup) semi-whipped cream

HOT MAPLE TAFFY MILK
- 600 ml (2⅓ cups) milk
- 75 ml (⅓ cup) maple taffy

Avoid putting this cake in the refrigerator before serving it.

Cakes: Heat the oven to 180°C (350°F). Sift all the dry ingredients together and put aside. Beat the cream, vegetable fat and sugar. Add the egg and beat to obtain a light texture. Add the vanilla. Incorporate the dry ingredients, alternating with the milk. Pour into greased and floured cupcake molds. Bake 45 to 50 min. in the oven at 180°C (350°F). Let sit 5 min. before cooling. Turn them over onto a grill and let cool completely before icing.

Fudge Sauce: Combine the cream, brown sugar and white sugar. Put into a saucepan and heat over medium-high heat until it just starts to boil. Stir well to obtain a uniform texture. Remove from heat and put aside.

Semi-Sour Semi-Whipped Cream: Combine the sour cream, allspice, icing sugar and semi-whipped cream. Stir well and put aside in the refrigerator.

Hot Maple Taffy Milk: In a saucepan, heat the milk and maple taffy over medium heat. As soon as the taffy has melted, turn off the heat and get ready to serve.

To Serve: Heat the cakes a few seconds in the oven or microwave oven. Place a cupcake on an individual plate. Garnish with a little semi-sour semi-whipped cream and fudge sauce. Serve with a glass of hot maple taffy milk.

Banana Crumble, Cinnamon Ice Cream, Red Wine Jelly and Mascarpone

Serves 4

Cinnamon Ice Cream: Heat the milk and cinnamon in a saucepan over medium-high heat. When it just starts to boil, remove from heat and let it soak up the cinnamon 7 min. Filter the milk with a China cap strainer and put aside. Whisk vigorously the egg yolks and sugar in a bowl to obtain a ribbon cream. Add the hot milk and stir 1 min. using a whisk. Pour into a saucepan and heat 4 min. over medium-high heat. Pour into another bowl and keep 3 hours in the freezer.

Mascarpone Cream: Combine the mascarpone cheese and the icing sugar in a food processor to obtain a smooth creamy texture. Put aside in the refrigerator.

Red Wine Jelly: In a saucepan, heat the wine, sugar, cinnamon and cloves 5 min. over medium heat. Remove from heat and let sit at room temperature. Let the mixture infuse 7 min. with the lid on, then filter. Soften the gelatine leaves in a bowl of cold water. Carefully wring out the water before placing them in the saucepan with the wine. Pour this liquid about 1 cm (½ in.) thick on a deep baking sheet and let cool 1 hour.

Crumble: Combine all the ingredients and spread 1 cm (½ in.) thick on a baking sheet. Bake 10 min. in the oven at 180°C (350°F). Let cool and break the dough apart with your hands.

To Serve: One hour before serving the dessert, combine the ice cream and the cinnamon in the food processor to obtain a cream. Put back in the freezer.

• When ready to serve, put a little cinnamon ice cream in parfait dishes. Put a little crumble on the ice cream. Top with a little mascarpone cream and add some cubes of red wine jelly. Insert the bananas cut in two and repeat the process to fill the dish. Serve immediately.

INGREDIENTS

CINNAMON ICE CREAM
- 250 ml (1 cup) milk
- 3 sticks of cinnamon
- 4 egg yolks
- 2 tablespoons sugar

MASCARPONE CREAM
- 200 ml (¾ cup) mascarpone cheese
- 1 tablespoon icing sugar

RED WINE JELLY
- 250 ml (1 cup) rather fruity red wine
- 2 teaspoons sugar
- 2 sticks of cinnamon
- 4 cloves
- 4 gelatine leaves

CRUMBLE
- 110 g (⅔ cup) flour
- 110 g (½ cup) butter
- 80 g (½ cup) icing sugar
- Pinch of salt
- 80 g (⅔ cup) chopped nuts

TO SERVE
- 8 miniature bananas

Thyme Shortbreads, Frozen Lemon-flavored Pineapple and Pernod Parfait

THYME SHORTBREADS

- 125 g (²/₃ cup) flour
- Pinch of lemon zest
- 80 g (¹/₃ cup) softened butter
- 80 g (¹/₃ cup) sugar
- 2 egg yolks
- Pinch of salt
- 1 teaspoon dried thyme powder

FROZEN PARFAIT

- 500 ml (2 cups) water
- 120 g (¹/₂ cup) sugar
- 3 egg yolks
- 175 ml (³/₄ cup) heavy cream (35 %)
- 75 ml (¹/₃ cup) Pernod

MACERATED PINEAPPLE BRUNOISE

- 125 ml (¹/₂ cup) water
- 2 tablespoons sugar
- Zest of one lemon
- One piece of pineapple, peeled and cut into a brunoise

THYME AND LEMON SYRUP

- 75 ml (¹/₃ cup) water
- 120 g (¹/₂ cup) sugar
- 1 teaspoon fresh thyme leaves
- Zest of one lemon

Make sure to renew your spices every year to get the maximum flavor out of your dishes.

Thyme Shortbreads: Combine the flour, lemon zest, butter, sugar, egg yolks and salt. Knead quickly, roll the dough into a ball and refrigerate 30 min. Preheat the oven to 200°C (400°F). Roll the dough to a thickness of 0.5 cm (¼ in.) and cut it into small 5 cm (2 in.) squares using a knife. Season the top with thyme. Place the shortbreads on a buttered baking sheet and bake in the oven 15 min. Put aside.

Frozen Parfait: Bring the water and sugar to a boil in a saucepan. After 1 min., remove immediately from the heat. Beat the egg yolks using an electric mixer to obtain a somewhat frothy cream. Add the very hot water slowly in a trickle and beat 7 min. to obtain a very light texture as that of a zabaglione. Pour into a larger bowl and incorporate the cream whipped to three-quarters stiff. Add the Pernod. Then pour onto a baking sheet with a depth of at least 4 cm (1½ in.) and keep 5 hours in the freezer. Cut into circles of 4 cm (1½ in.) using a cutter and put back in the freezer.

Macerated Pineapple Brunoise: Bring the water, sugar and zest to a boil in a saucepan. When it just starts to boil, pour onto the pineapple and keep in the refrigerator until ready to serve.

Thyme and Lemon Syrup: Bring the water and sugar to a boil in a saucepan. Remove from heat and add the thyme and lemon zest. Pour into a bowl and put aside.

To Serve: Put a shortbread on a dessert plate. Cover with a frozen parfait circle. Repeat the process once again and finish with one or two shortbreads. Garnish with the pineapple brunoise with a little syrup on the side. Serve a little pineapple brunoise in a spoon on the side.

Lychee and Strawberry Pastry With
White Chocolate Mousse

Serves 4

**Soak the strawberries in a little white port
before preparing the plates.**

White Chocolate Mousse: Whip the cream halfway. Melt the chocolate in a double boiler, then incorporate the whipped cream in two steps. Do not overstir or the cream will turn. Refrigerate at least 1 hour.

Pastry: Spread the phyllo dough into two layers, sprinkling a little sugar between each layer. Cut into the desired shape and bake 8 to 10 min. in the oven at 180°C (350°F). Let cool.

Fruit Cocktail: Combine the canned lychees and strawberries and put aside.

To Serve: Put a spoonful of white chocolate mousse on individual plates and top with the fruit cocktail. Add the layers of phyllo dough. Repeat the process. Garnish each portion with a fresh lychee fruit and half a strawberry before serving.

PREPARATION

INGREDIENTS

WHITE CHOCOLATE MOUSSE
- 250 ml (1 cup) heavy cream (35 %)
- 120 g (4 oz.) white chocolate

PASTRY
- 1 package phyllo dough
- Sugar

FRUIT COCKTAIL
- 1 can lychees, drained and quartered
- 200 g (1 cup) strawberries, quartered

TO SERVE
- 4 fresh lychee fruits
- 2 fresh strawberries, cut in two

Glossary

Al dente
Italian cooking term to describe pasta cooked until still somewhat firm or vegetables that are firm to the bite.

Aragula
A small strong-flavored leaf used in salads. A traditional part of mesclun.

Arctic Char
Fresh-water fish resembling salmon.

Blanch
To cook vegetables in boiling water a few minutes to soften them or make them less bitter.

Blin
A small pancake from Russia served as an hors d'oeuvre or as a dessert.

Brandade
A purée similar to mashed potatoes prepared using cod flesh, olive oil and milk.

Brunoise
A technique for cutting food into small cubes of 1 to 2 cm (½ to 1 in.).

Carpaccio
An entrée made of fine strips of marinated raw beef or vegetables.

Ceviche
A South American dish made of raw fish marinated in lemon juice.

Chanterelle
A type of mushroom.

Chayote
A type of squash that can be served raw in a salad or cooked.

Darphin
A small vegetable patty grilled on the outside and tender inside.

Deglaze
To dissolve the particles remaining in a pan using a liquid to obtain a sauce.

Emulsion
Result obtained after combining two liquids that do not mix, for example oil and vinegar, when making vinaigrettes or sauces.

Espelette Pepper
Hot red pepper from the Basque region. It can be used whole, in a paste or as a powder.

Farigoule
Type of wild thyme from the Mediterranean region.

Granite
Italian-style sorbet.

Gremolata
Mixture of chopped garlic, lemon zest, parsley or other fresh herb.

Macerate
To soak food in a liquid (aromatic oil, alcohol) so that the aroma permeates it.

Mascarpone
A soft white cheese whose texture resembles that of firm whipped cream. It is rich in fat and is closely related to ricotta.

Mesclun
A mixed salad containing fresh baby shoots (corn salad, escarole, oak leaves, etc.).

Monbazillac
A sweet white wine similar to a sauternes.

Orzo

Small rice-shaped pasta.

Pancetta

Italian deli meat made from pork. When grilled, it can be used to spice up salads or omelets.

Pine Nut

An edible seed from the Mediterranean umbrella pine used in salads, desserts and basil pesto.

Polenta

Boiled cornmeal.

Pont Couvert

Cheese from Québec made in the Eastern Townships.

Portobello

Type of mushroom with a large cap.

Ramequin

Small flameproof container used for serving entrées or desserts, hot or cold, in individual portions.

Ratte

Oblong, kidney-shaped yellow potato.

Ravigote

Somewhat spicy sauce or vinaigrette.

Risotto

Italian rice preparation served with various accompaniments. The rice is cooked first of all in a fatty substance and then put in a broth that is evaporated in a sequence of steps.

Rouelle

Cut of meat, fish or vegetables in round rather thick slices.

Sweat

To heat food over low heat to rid it of its water.

Tatin

Name in memory of the Tatin sisters who invented the "upside down" apple pie. The term also designates a turned-over vegetable dish.

Tomme

Goat milk cheese from South East France or cow milk cheese made in Savoy and Switzerland.

Turban Squash

Squash weighing 1 to 4 kg (2 to 9 lb.) rich in water, grown in certain tropical countries.

Victor et Berthold

Raw milk cheese from Québec made in the Lanaudière region.

Violet Mustard

A recipe originating from Brive in the 16th century. Its purple color comes from the grape must, wine and vinegar used in its making.

Yuzu

Green fruit with a dimpled rind similar to a lime used frequently in Thai cuisine.

Index

Detailed index

Printed in Canada
at Imprimeries Transcontinental Inc.